CONSTITUTIONALISM, DEMOCRACY, AND FOREIGN AFFAIRS

For Suzanne Stratford
with all good wishes

Louis Henkin

11/19/97

Constitutionalism, Democracy, and Foreign Affairs

LOUIS HENKIN

COLUMBIA UNIVERSITY PRESS
New York

COLUMBIA UNIVERSITY PRESS
New York   Oxford
Copyright © 1990 Columbia University Press
All rights reserved

Library of Congress Cataloging-in-Publication Data

Henkin, Louis.
Constitutionalism, democracy, and foreign affairs / Louis Henkin.
p. cm.
"Essays . . . from the Cooley lectures delivered at the University
of Michigan Law School in November 1988"—Pref.
Includes bibliographical references.
ISBN 0-231-07228-7
1. United States—Foreign relations—Law and legislation.
2. United States—Constitutional law.   I. Title.
KF4651.H447   1990
342.73′0412—dc20
[347.302412]   90-1419
CIP

Casebound editions of Columbia University Press books are Smyth-sewn
and printed on permanent and durable acid-free paper

Printed in the United States of America

c   10 9 8 7 6 5 4 3 2

Contents

■

v

Preface

■

The essays in this volume derive from the Cooley Lectures delivered at the University of Michigan Law School in November 1988. I devoted those lectures, prepared and delivered during the years of celebration of the Bicentennial of the United States Constitution, to a highly controversial yet neglected aspect of constitutional jurisprudence, that which governs the conduct of United States foreign relations.

Running through these essays is the question frequently voiced but hardly explored: Is our two-hundred-year-old Constitution satisfactory for its third century? That is a big question requiring big answers, and I have not addressed its larger dimensions. For example, I do not consider whether we should move to a parliamentary system or whether we should abandon federalism. Nor have I addressed less radical but nonetheless major adjustments in our present system, such as a six-year term for the President or four-year terms for members of the House of Representatives. I have assumed that we will continue with the kind of government we have, commonly described as the presidential system (more accurately, the congressional-presidential system), and I have assumed its continued existence generally in its current form. Is that government, I ask, satisfactory for the conduct of our foreign relations in the decades ahead? In that undertaking I consider—as suggested by the title of these lectures—the relevance for constitutional jurisprudence of our political ideology, of the principles of constitutionalism with which we began and the principles of the democracy we have finally become. For me that perspective has particular significance for foreign affairs. I leave its possible relevance to constitutional jurisprudence generally for another day and for others.

Chapters 1 to 3 are adaptations of the 1988 Cooley Lectures as delivered. I have added an introductory essay and a chapter on individual rights to develop ideas to which I had only alluded in the lectures and a postscript to sum up.

I am grateful to the Faculty of Law of the University of Michigan, which invited me to deliver these lectures, inspired me to think further on their subject, and afforded generous and gracious hospitality when they were delivered. I am grateful to others who helped me prepare the lectures for publication, notably Grace Shelton, J. D. 1989, Columbia Law School and Elizabeth Martin, A.B. 1989, Columbia University.

Introduction

∎

During these Bicentennial years, we frequently have been reminded of Gladstone's famous compliment to the United States Constitution and its framers: the Constitution, he said, is "the most wonderful work ever struck off at a given time by the brain and purpose of man."[1] Americans have been celebrating the Bicentennial in that spirit, with visible pride and audible self-satisfaction, and with worshipful appreciation of the wisdom and prescience of the framers. Infrequent reminders that the Constitution which they framed was the product of its time, that it reflected some values we now recall with deep embarrassment — slavery, limited suffrage, the subordination of women—are decried as spoilsport. Few have apparently considered this to be the time even to recall that in important details the Constitution that the founders framed was not a perfect realization of ideals and principles, but as Charles and Mary Beard described it, "a mosaic of everyone's second choices."[2] Not many, in the academy or in public life, have asked whether the Constitution might require tuning if not overhaul for its third century.

1

Students of foreign affairs, in particular, might voice a more sober mood. They could not help but note that during these Bicentennial years Americans breathed the Iran-contra miasma; followed with pained incomprehension the struggles of President and Congress over Nicaragua and her neighbors; heard the President and the Senate shout disagreement over presidential authority to interpret (reinterpret) the Anti-Ballistic Missile (ABM) Treaty; and watched the United States slip into the Persian Gulf and the Iran-Iraq War. During these years many have wondered who was in charge in Washington. The country has not verged on constitutional crisis, but few have been moved to declare that the constitutional arrangements for conducting the foreign affairs of the United States are worthy of celebration.

Constitutional uncertainties have troubled the conduct of foreign relations from the beginning, at least since Washington's Neutrality Proclamation (1795) and the Jay Treaty (1794). In a famous opinion in 1952, Supreme Court Justice Robert H. Jackson gave authoritative expression to those perplexities, describing a "twilight zone" in which the distribution of power between President and Congress was uncertain (or their powers concurrent).[3] The conduct of foreign affairs has been the principal occupant of that twilight zone for two hundred years, engendering the most intractable issues of constitutional law. For reasons lawyers know — principally the Supreme Court's jurisprudence of not hearing cases, from the constitutional requirement of case or controversy to prudential avoidance of "political questions" — the courts have resolved few of these perennial foreign affairs issues. Indeed, judicial abstention may have perpetuated and even extended and aggravated uncertainties and has created a judicial twilight zone of uncertainty as well (see chapter 3).

I have emphasized constitutional uncertainties. But much constitutional controversy in foreign affairs springs from what the Constitution clearly prescribes. For a lively example, friction between President and Senate in the exercise of their shared authority in the making of treaties has agitated our political universe from President Washington's time through Polk's, Cleveland's, Theodore Roosevelt's, and Wilson's and in between, again in 1987 over the ABM Treaty, and in 1988 over the INF Treaty; there is little reason to expect that such friction will be absent during President Bush's years in office and thereafter. Built-in friction apart, students of constitutional politics might suggest that major constitutional tensions result also from deep dissatisfaction with what the framers wrought and from what time has done to what they laid down. Much has changed since governmental authority in foreign affairs was allocated in 1787. The intimate Congress of the framers' generation has been transformed into a complex of five hundred members with numerous committees and subcommittees and many thousands of staff. The President has become the presidency, the executive branch, with a bureaucracy of millions, all of them exercising the President's constitutional authority. Over the centuries, each branch of the federal government has aggrandized its constitutional powers and has developed large extraconstitutional powers, the consequences of political parties and patronage, of size and complexities, of the growth of the United States and of a changing world. The judiciary—Alexander Hamilton's "least dangerous"[4] branch—has grown from a handful of circuit riders to a small army that has achieved judicial supremacy. Yet, with all these transformations, the original constitutional allocations of authority remain. Presidents in particular, I think, often see the constitutional blueprint as out-of-date for the country we have become in the world in which we live. Congress often marvels at the shape the Constitution has assumed and sometimes yearns for earlier simplicity and—especially—for executive modesty. The courts are often dismayed by the authority they have acquired and are asked to exercise.

I do not come, then, to praise the constitutional dispositions governing the conduct of foreign relations. But neither do I come to bury them. The old organs are remarkably vigorous, and we have done marvelously well with them; at worst, we have muddled through. But constitutional uncertainties, constitutional friction, and constitutional dissatisfaction breed constitutional controversy, instability, and occasional crisis, confusing the student of the Constitution and troubling the citizen. If the Constitution does not require new organs, is it time for a checkup and some rehabilitation? If the Constitution does not require radical amendment, it may be time to attend anew to how we interpret, apply and implement the Constitution we have.

In these essays I attempt to define the constitutional uncertainties, frictions, and dissatisfactions that beset us in the conduct of foreign affairs. I offer my views as to what constitutional text seems to mean and what the framers intended, what has happened during two hundred years to the system they projected, and whether what we have now conforms to ancestral precepts and future needs. I suggest that what we need for the third century is constitutional construction that will recommit us to the principles of constitutionalism with which we began and reflect the democracy we have become.

In that light I look at issues between Congress and President, including that congeries of issues commonly mispackaged as "war powers" (chapter 1), relate those concerns to competition for power within the Treaty Power (chapter 2), and address the role of the courts in the foreign affairs of a republic that has become a democracy, a constitutional democracy (chapter 3). Finally, I consider issues of individual rights arising out of our foreign relations and how they might be resolved by a "community of conscience" whose respect for rights is its hallmark and its pride (chapter 4).

CONSTITUTION, REPUBLIC, AND DEMOCRACY

■ It is relevant to recall the framers' political ideology.

Three streams fed the framers' thought. They followed in British constitutional history, their political heritage, much of which they took as given. They were raised on English and European ideas—on Locke, filtered through Blackstone, and on Montesquieu. They drew on their own experience both before and since independence. All these strands were subject to be modified by political compromise, but there was no compromise of their fundamental ideological commitment.

The framers were committed to inherent rights, to social contract, to constitutionalism, to republicanism.

The state constitutions, and the later United States Constitution, reflected the framers' theory of government, the self-evident truths that Jefferson encapsulated in famous, ringing phrases: "That all men are created equal. That they are endowed by their Creator with certain unalienable rights, that among these are Life, Liberty and the Pursuit of Happiness. That to secure these rights, governments are instituted among men, deriving their just powers from the consent of the governed." Ultimate authority, sovereignty, resides in the people: legitimate government derives from and rests on their consent. Both state and federal governments were instituted "to secure these rights."

CONSTITUTION

■ A legitimate political society is based on the consent of the people, reflected in a social contract among the people to institute a government. The social contract generally takes the form of a constitution, which also establishes a framework of government and a blueprint for its institutions. By the constitutional contract the people consent to be governed. The officers of the government-to-be later commit themselves to respect the constitutional blueprint and its limitations.

For the generations of the framers, a constitution went with government; if there was to be a government, the need for a constitution went without saying. England, from which they had separated, had a constitution even if it was not written or not written in one place, but was the sum of royal decrees, charters, acts of parliament, other instruments, customs, and traditions that established the system and institutions of government. As Bolingbroke put it:

> "By constitution we mean, whenever we speak with propriety and exactness, that assemblage of laws, institutions and customs, derived from certain fixed principles of reason, directed to certain fixed objects of public good, that compose the general system, according to which the community hath agreed to be governed. ... We call this a good government, when ... the whole administration of public affairs is wisely pursued, and with a *strict conformity to the principles and objects* of the constitution."[5]

The newly independent states were building new political societies and therefore needed new constitutions.

Even before it adopted the Declaration of Independence in Philadelphia in 1776, the Continental Congress resolved that each former colony, now to be an independent state, should adopt a state government.[6] And so, immediately after independence, each of the thirteen states established its own new constitution and its new state government. In 1787, again in Philadelphia, the delegates who had assembled to amend the Articles of Confederation decided that a more perfect union required not confederation but a new central government and, therefore, that the Articles must be replaced by a constitution. The Convention of 1787 therefore came to be called the Constitutional Convention, and the document that issued from their deliberations begins: "We the people . . . do ordain and establish this Constitution for the United States of America." Like the constitutions of the states, the United States Constitution was a contract among the people to establish a new government and a contract between the people and the government-to-be, the people consenting to be governed according to the forms and subject to the terms prescribed, the government being committed to respect those prescriptions.

CONSTITUTIONALISM

■ Every constitution sets forth a framework of government, but contrary to common assumptions, a constitution does not necessarily bespeak a framework that conforms to principles of republicanism or democracy, of respect for human rights or any other particular values. Many a constitution is only a description of the government that is, or a manifesto, or a hope or a program for the future.[7] Some constitutions contain no bill of rights. Some constitutions have no significance as law, surely not as supreme law. Some that proclaim they are supreme law are not so in fact, if only because they are not attended to or enforced or because they can readily be amended by political authorities. To be sure, even a constitution that has all of these weaknesses implies some limitations on government; the fact of a constitution suggests some rule of law, some restraint on autarchy and caprice.

For the framers, a constitution meant more. It implied "constitutionalism"—that the government to be instituted shall be constrained by the constitution and shall govern only according to its terms and subject to its limitations, only with agreed powers and for agreed purposes.

For the framers, constitutionalism also meant something more. From European thought, the framers' generation, for whom Jefferson wrote, drew a commitment to government for limited purposes—the minimal government of the liberal state. Free men instituted government and agreed to be governed by it only for the purpose of securing their life, liberty, and property and other rights. The individual retains these rights even against the people's representatives in government.*

* In this respect, the framers' ideology differed markedly from prominent European thought and from English constitutional doctrine. In Rousseau's social contract, individuals came together to

We speak of our constitutional rights, but for the framers rights did not derive from or depend on the Constitution. Rights antedated any constitution, antedated society, antedated government. The purpose of government was to secure the rights that in principle men and women enjoyed before there was any government, rights with which they are endowed by the Creator. In agreeing to form a society, individuals agreed to give up some of their liberty and property to their representatives for the purposes of governing. But the people—the inhabitants taken together—retained the ultimate authority, and the individual continued to enjoy rights against the representatives of the people. A constitution may articulate the rights that the individual retains and remind government that it is to respect them; hence, for example, "Congress shall make no law abridging the freedom" of the press. But the individual had that freedom before the Constitution, and government is obliged to respect that freedom and his/her other retained rights even if they were not enumerated or even alluded to in the Constitution.

[margin, handwritten: Presumably this forms a basis for the argument for a right to abortion.]

The framers' constitutionalism was committed to limited government in yet another sense. They were satisfied that government will remain limited only if the powers of government were separated. Legislative power was to be separated from executive power and both from judicial power. In addition, there were to be checks and balances among the branches.

[margin, handwritten: Well no that doesn't make sense. It might be a right, but unless Const recognizes it, there's]

In sum, American constitutionalism implies a government subject to the Constitution; it implies limited government, government with agreed powers for agreed purposes, subject to the rule of law; it implies fractionalized authority to prevent concentration of power and the danger of tyranny. Constitutionalism implies also the reservation of a large private domain and retained rights for every individual. (It did not, I think, mean commitment to romantic libertarianism or formalistic adherence to separation of powers, though the United States Supreme Court has sometimes insisted on it.) [8] And constitutionalism

[margin, handwritten: no indication that "gov't shall make no law restricting it."]

form "the nation" and sovereignty was in the nation. Thereafter the individual retains no rights; he/she finds his/her liberty and property secured by the general will of the nation in which every individual is fully and equally represented. Unlike Rousseau, Locke postulated a social contract under which the individual retains rights, but English constitutional instruments and English constitutional practice generally refer to the rights of "the people," not of individuals. The people's rights were based on contract between Parliament and king and were protected through law. More in the spirit of Rousseau than of Locke, the individual English citizen had to find protection in laws enacted by the people's representatives. Neither conservatives (such as Burke), nor progressives (e.g., Bentham) believed in natural rights or accepted any rights against Parliament, the people's representatives.

may require an independent institution such as a judiciary to assure that government will not deviate from the constitutional prescriptions, in particular to assure against concentration of power and violation of individual rights.

REPUBLIC AND DEMOCRACY

■ The framers established a constitutional republic and the Constitution they framed explicitly required the United States to "guarantee to every State in this Union a Republican Form of Government."* *Republic* had no clearer definition in the days of the framers than it has now. Etymologically, *republic* was generally equivalent to *commonwealth* or *common weal,* but that itself implied nothing as to the source of political authority or the character of government. As in ancient Rome, however, for the framers republic was contrasted with monarchy. But a republic was not merely a rejection of hereditary rule, of titles of nobility and hierarchies of estates and classes. For the framers, as in ancient Rome, a republic meant that supreme power resided in the people, that the source of authority was the people, and that government was created by the people and was responsible to it.

[*Instead of god .* — handwritten margin note]

James Madison explained:

> If we resort for a criterion to the different principles on which different forms of government are established, we may define a republic to be, or at least may bestow that name on, a government which derives all its powers directly or indirectly from the great body of the people, and is administered by persons holding their offices during pleasure for a limited period, or during good behavior. It is *essential* to such a government that it be derived from the great body of the society, not from an

*U.S. Constitution, Art. IV, sec. 4. In *The Federalist Papers,* no. 39, James Madison said:

The first question that offers itself is whether the general form and aspect of the government be strictly republican. It is evident that no other form would be reconcilable with the genius of the people of America; with the fundamental principles of the Revolution; or with that honorable determination which animates every votary of freedom to rest all our political experiments on the capacity of mankind for self-government. If the plan of the convention, therefore, be found to depart from the republican character, its advocates must abandon it as no longer defensible.

What, then, are the distinctive characters of the republican form? Were an answer to this question to be sought, not by recurring to principles but in the application of the term by political writers to the constitutions of different States, no satisfactory one would ever be found. . . . These examples, which are nearly as dissimilar to each other as to a genuine republic, show the extreme inaccuracy with which the term has been used in political disquisitions.

inconsiderable proportion or a favored class of it; otherwise a handful of tyrannical nobles, exercising their oppressions by a delegation of their powers, might aspire to the rank of republicans and claim for their government the honorable title of republic. It is *sufficient* for such a government that the persons administering it be appointed, either directly or indirectly, by the people; and that they hold their appointments by either of the tenures just specified; otherwise every government in the United States, as well as every other popular government that has been or can be well organized or well executed, would be degraded from the republican character.*

i.e. represent. democ. is ok as a form of republicanism.

REPRESENTATIVE GOVERNMENT

■ To the extent that in a republic the people were sovereign and governed, a republic was also democratic. But the framers distinguished sharply between a republic and a democracy. For them, democracy implied direct popular government, with decisions made by vote of the people in assembly; a republic implied representative government. Government by the people directly, by the people assembled, was of course impractical if not impossible for any society of substantial population. But the framers' objection to direct popular government ran deeper. The framers believed in representative government. They thought that representative government was better government, more conducive to the common weal. The people should govern through the best among them. The framers feared the common man,[9] particularly in public and in large groups, where he or she can be manipulated by demagogues. They also saw direct democracy as prone to factional- *?* ism.

The officers of government were to represent the people, and representatives, Madison said, should be selected by the people. But the people could select their representatives directly or indirectly; the fram-

* *The Federalist Papers*, no. 39 (emphasis in original). Madison continued:

According to the constitution of every State in the Union, some or other of the officers of government are appointed indirectly only by the people. According to most of them, the chief magistrate himself is so appointed. And according to one, this mode of appointment is extended to one of the coordinate branches of the legislature. According to all the constitutions, also, the tenure of the highest offices is extended to a definite period, and in many instances, both within the legislative and executive departments, to a period of years. According to the provisions of most of the constitutions, again, as well as according to the most respectable and received opinions on the subject, the members of the judiciary department are to retain their offices by the firm tenure of good behavior.

See also *The Federalist Papers*, no. 10 (J. Madison).

ers saw no particular preference for direct elections and indeed, as is evident from the constitution they framed, they seemed to prefer indirect selection. Only the House of Representatives was explicitly representative—only its members are called "representatives"; even in the election of these representatives the qualifications for voting were left to the states where they were determined by legislatures not wholly chosen directly by the people. The framers perhaps saw the Senate, too, as representing the people; Senators, however, were not to be elected by the people but "chosen by the legislature" of the state.* The President, too, presumably represented the people, but he was elected even less directly than the Senate, by electors appointed by the state "in such manner as the legislature thereof may direct."

LIMITED SUFFRAGE

■ For the framers, government by the people did not mean by all the people. Slaves and even free blacks, women, and persons without sufficient property were not eligible to vote, whether for the delegates to the state conventions that ratified the United States Constitution or later for members of the House of Representatives or for the popularly elected branch of the state legislature that helped determine the qualifications for voting for the House of Representatives and the selection of the President and Senators. It has been estimated that some 5 percent of the population voted for delegates to the conventions to ratify the Constitution,[10] the instrument beginning: "We the people . . ." Not many more voted, directly or indirectly, for any of the representatives, in the states or later in the federal government.

Republicanism, then, was committed to the sovereignty of the people and the consent of the governed, but effectively the sovereign people and the consenting governed were a small percentage of the population. Republicanism was committed to representative, accountable government, but only some of the different "representatives" were elected directly by the voters and could be held accountable by them.

---

*Many saw the Senate as representing not the people but the states, since each state had two Senators regardless of its population. And the Senate was not "popular" but "aristocratic."[9] Members of the Senate were fewer and had longer terms. The Senate and the House of Representatives had generally equal powers in legislation, but the Senate also had special additional powers, in consenting to treaties, in confirming appointments.

Republicanism seemed to value checks and balances, but the checks and balances were to be applied in large part by officials not elected by the people and accountable to them. And whether elections for an office were direct or indirect, the eligible voters were only a small part of the people represented by that office.

Even in 1787, however, *democracy* was an appealing word, and many among the framers did not wish to appear antidemocratic or even undemocratic. At the end, the Federalists "sought to cover their aristocratic document with a democratic mantle."[11] In any event, during two hundred years conceptions of republicanism and of democracy have changed and merged. The basic differences that the framers perceived between democracy and republicanism have disappeared: democracy, too, is now seen as representative, and ours is a representative democracy. (For the framers, *representative* democracy would have been an oxymoron. (See p. 9.) In general, the exaltation of republicanism as the characteristic of good government has been replaced by commitment to democracy.

That commitment has also been enriched and refined. We have extended our definition of *the people*. We have had further thoughts on representation and on accountability. Although direct government continues to be recognized as generally impossible, some public participation has come to be seen as desirable and conducive to more authentic democracy.

Most important, all the people are now eligible to vote.* Slowly, though in quantum leaps, suffrage, once very limited, became virtually universal. Disqualificatory barriers fell one at a time — race in 1870, gender in 1920, property (via the poll or other taxes) in 1964, age (for those over eighteen) in 1971).† In 1970 Congress suspended literacy tests.[12] Then, all barriers fell when the Supreme Court established universal suffrage by finding that the constitutional right to the equal protection of the laws included the equal right of all to an equal vote.[13]

We the people who ordained the Constitution in 1789 were a small percentage of the 3 million inhabitants; today we the people who accept and support the Constitution as our constitution and give our consent to be governed are virtually all the citizens among the 250

---

*Subject to constitutional limitations, eligibility to vote is determined by the states and they have limited the right to vote to citizens. But all persons born in the United States are citizens and all aliens admitted to residence are made eligible for citizenship by relatively unburdensome procedures.

†Amendments XV, XIX, XXIV, XXVI, respectively.

million inhabitants of the country. All of us are represented and represented directly.* Nominally, formally, the President is still elected by
appointed electors, but the electoral college is the barest formality, and
it is not false or misleading to say that the President is elected by the
people, although that vote is weighted along state lines. We have rarely
—and now not for a hundred years—elected a President who did not
receive a majority of the votes cast, and we decry and fear that possibil-
ity because it would be undemocratic; a "minority" President would
be evidence of the failure of democracy.

Wow. [handwritten annotation]

*There's a whole essay in that phrase, considering what's
resulted after our particular failure (on so many levels) in 2000.* [handwritten annotation]

IMPLICATIONS OF DEMOCRACY

■ We are a democracy because we now have universal suffrage, but
we have become a democracy without conscious conversion from republicanism to democracy. The extensions of the right to vote were—
in form and in principle—expressions of nondiscrimination and of
greater equality, not of a commitment to popular sovereignty, to government by all the people. When the Supreme Court impelled us to
universal suffrage it did so on principles of equal protection, disallow-
ing discrimination as to voting as elsewhere, not on the basis of
democratic theory, of the implications of the self-evident truths of the
social contract and the sovereignty of the people.

Democracy is not simply a right to vote. Universal suffrage and
direct elections, I suggest, have changed the character and content of
our democracy and of our representation. Now popular sovereignty
and representative government, the foundations of our government in
principle for two hundred years, have become a reality. Now all of us
are represented; now our agents must be responsive to all of us, are
responsible to all of us, accountable to all of us. Now all of us are "we
the people," parties to the social contract; now all of us are the governed whose consent is necessary to make our government legitimate.
Our commitment to democracy ought to permeate our system of
government. In principle, our move from aristocratic republic to representative democracy might well call for complete rethinking of our

---

*In a sense, the Senate still represents states, not people, since all states have equal representation
regardless of differences in population, but seventy-five years ago we moved to direct election of
senators. The inhabitants of the District of Columbia are not represented in the Senate (or in the
House of Representatives), but they do vote for electors for President pursuant to the Twenty-third
Amendment.

system of government and its institutions. Surely it is not inappropriate to assimilate that development into our jurisprudence and to invoke our democracy to guide us in the construction of our Constitution. There is no authoritative definition of democracy even today. Universal suffrage may be a necessary index, but that may define anything from direct rule by frequent popular initiative and referendum to infrequent plebiscites on a feared (or even a popular) autocrat. Universal suffrage establishes an acceptable measure of democracy if it reflects or accompanies the essence of democracy. Among its key elements, I suggest, are authentic and effective representation of the voters and authentic and effective accountability, even—to the extent possible—some measure of citizen participation.

Representation, accountability, and participation can be more or less authentic and more or less significant. Effective representation is most important, since it is the expression of popular sovereignty and the surrogate for direct popular self-government. One need not stop to reargue Edmund Burke's famous position[14] that a representative owes to his constituents only that he act in their best interests by his best lights, not that he determine and do their bidding. With increased sophistication and improved communication, the distinction between the two may have been narrowed and blurred. Our theory of representation now, I believe, requires responsiveness to the people's needs as well as attention to their communicated desires and responsibility for their welfare as well as accountability for their trust. Accountability requires being subject not only to periodic judgment at election time, but to frequent and candid communication to those represented. Democracy keeps in mind that representation is a surrogate for governance by the people and that it can be enriched by citizen participation, by reciprocal communication and consultation.

The framers' republicanism meant partial, weak representation, indirect election, and consequently weak responsibility, weak accountability, and virtually no popular participation. Our democracy means universal suffrage and should mean stronger representation, responsiveness, responsibility, accountability, and a modicum of participation. The move from a partly representative republic with largely indirect representation to universal suffrage and direct representation, I conclude, ought to be reflected in our institutions and in our procedures of government. I do not think they have been.

Our transformation to a representative democracy has not brought any constitutional change in our governance. The United States has been transformed, the federal government has been transformed, Congress and the presidency have been transformed, but except for the move to direct election of Senators, now seventy-five years ago, the Constitution has not been amended to modify the framework of government, the distribution of governmental authority among the branches, or the powers and functions of any branch.* Those who occupy the institutions of government — the two Houses of Congress, the Presidency, the judiciary — are selected much as they were two hundred years ago.† The powers of the different branches remain textually and formally the same. We have not modified or reexamined our federalism, our separation of powers, our checks and balances, or our retained individual rights. Any redistribution in the powers of the political branches has been not by formal amendment, not according to some theory of democracy, but extraconstitutionally in response to political forces operating in a growing, spreading, changing country. Expanding suffrage did not seem to mean greater, better citizen participation, more authentic or more effective representation in fact. Officials did not become significantly more responsible and did not produce government that is more responsive to popular views or needs; it did not make them more or better accountable.

Of course we have come a long way from what the framers provided and intended, without formal amendment. Our federalism has been radically revised by application and reconstruction of the Commerce Clause, the spending power, and other powers of Congress to reflect the transformations in our size, population, economy, transportation, and communication. The distribution of authority between President and Congress prevails, but an innocent clause authorizing/requiring the President to recommend to congressional "Consideration such Measures as he shall judge necessary and expedient," has made the executive the principal author of national legislation and policy and of a trillion dollar budget. Separation of powers and checks and balances have been reshaped by the emergence of the administrative state and the administrative "fourth branch" of government. The judiciary has become supreme. Individual rights have been extended here and narrowed there by constitutional interpretation. But in all that constitu-

---

*The Civil War amendments and several later Amendments gave Congress the power to implement those Amendments, but, in principle, such new powers for Congress were not at the expense of the other branches of the federal government, but of the states.
† In the case of the Senate, as modified by the 17th Amendment.

tional change, in the calibration, interpretation, and reinterpretation, I have not seen much thought given to the fact that we remain committed to constitutionalism and we have become committed to a fuller democracy.

It is difficult to believe that, assuming continued commitment to our congressional-presidential system, we would decide today to distribute governmental authority in the way the framers did and bequeathed. Assuming our continued commitment to constitutionalism, to federalism, to separation of powers and checks and balances, to individual rights, how different should our blueprint of government be now that we are a representative democracy instead of the republic of our ancestors? And if our commitment to constitutionalism includes loyalty to the text we have inherited (unless we were prepared to modify it by the difficult amendment process it prescribes), ought we not at least fill its gaps and interpret its ambiguities to satisfy better the elements of democracy as well as constitutionalism—limited government, the rule of law, representation, responsibility, accountability, participation?

■ Concern for the adequacy of our two-hundred-year-old blueprint is a challenge to every aspect of our constitutional governance. The framers' commitment to constitutionalism, and our commitment to democracy, I will suggest, should shape our constitutional jurisprudence in the "twilight zone" where the distribution of authority between Congress and the President is uncertain (or their powers concurrent) and where constitutional confrontation is our daily lot. Is the allocation of legislative powers wholly to Congress and executive power to the President adequate and satisfactory now that all of us vote for both and both are representative in their different ways and degrees? Is the distribution between federal and state government as propounded by the framers still satisfactory now that we are an authentic democracy both in our state and federal governments? Would we today ordain our current federalism, our separation of powers, our checks and balances, our judicial review, our accommodation between individual rights and the powers of government? Individual rights and judicial review, our constitutional hallmarks, might well look different in an authentic democracy, even a constitutional democracy.

I have not attempted to write all the terms of the marriage of our old commitment to constitutionalism with our new commitment to democracy or to explore the implications of that marriage for constitutional law and jurisprudence generally. I shall suggest what I think to be the relevance of constitutionalism and of democracy to the governance of our foreign affairs.

1

TENSION IN THE TWILIGHT ZONE: CONGRESS AND THE PRESIDENT

■

Issues as to the respective constitutional authority of Congress and the President dominate the constitutional jurisprudence of foreign affairs. There are deep differences as to what the Constitution prescribes and what the framers intended. There is also, I think, some significant unhappiness—principally by Presidents—with the original allocations of power to the branches, and steady pressure to redistribute them.

The principal issues between the President and Congress in foreign affairs appear in the daily newspapers. President Reagan sends marines to Lebanon and troops to Grenada, mines Nicaraguan harbors, bombs Libya. Members of Congress challenge his constitutional authority to take these and other actions and demand that the President comply with the War Powers Resolution—but Presidents claim the resolution is unconstitutional. Congress legislates to regulate "covert activities," sometimes known as "dirty tricks," and the executive branch flouts the law, as in the Iran-Contra disgrace, with some suggestion that the law was not constitutional. (I leave for later the newspaper-reported battles over President Carter's termination of the Defense Treaty with Taiwan and President Reagan's reinterpretation of the ABM Treaty.)

These and other issues agitate our polity and confuse our jurisprudence. They are instances of a large uncertainty about the distribution of authority in the determination of foreign policy which is virtually unknown in our domestic governance. There is dispute as to the constitutional authority of the President and particularly his authority to use the armed forces without congressional authorization; there is dispute as to the authority of Congress to regulate presidential action. This is Justice Jackson's twilight zone (see p. 12), and there is tension and tug-of-war within it.

■ *The Text.* The Constitution we are expounding is a written constitution, and it is holy writ. We begin with the text, even if we sometimes come out pretty far from where we began, or find in the text what is visible only to infallible Supreme Court Justices.

The authors of the Constitution framed a more perfect union by distributing authority between the federal government and the states and by allocating federal authority among three branches of the new government. In general, the Constitution performs both divisions simultaneously: it grants power to the federal government by allocating it to one of the branches. As regards foreign affairs, however, it is accepted that the delegation to the federal government was intended to be virtually complete,[1] although the enumerated allocations to the political branches leave much unsaid.

Some prescriptions of the Constitution are explicit, clear, and difficult to dispute. The Constitution gives Congress "all legislative power herein granted," in foreign as in domestic affairs. No legislative power is given to any other branch of the federal government.*

Of the powers that the Constitution expressly confers upon the federal government and allocates to its branches, some are related directly to foreign affairs. Congress has the power to regulate commerce with foreign nations, to define offenses against the law of nations, to declare war. Other expressed powers of Congress have applications and implications for foreign affairs: the power to tax and spend for the common defense and the general welfare, to raise and support

---

*Lawmaking by treary and judicial lawmaking are minor and incidental to other purposes and functions of the treaty makers and the courts.

an army and navy, to borrow and to coin money, to establish a postal system, to make laws necessary and proper to carry out their other powers and the powers of other branches of the federal government. Some federal powers are expressly allocated to the President: The President can make treaties (with the advice and consent of the Senate). He can appoint ambassadors and other officers, including those engaged in the conduct of foreign affairs. He shall receive ambassadors and other public ministers. He is designated Commander in Chief of the armed forces.

It has been said that "the draftsmen could not often assemble the words of a sentence without some reference to the foreign affairs of the little republic to be."[2] Yet as regards foreign affairs, the text appears today to be strangely incomplete. The term *foreign affairs* is not in the Constitution; the conception of foreign affairs reflected in the constitutional dispositions seems incredibly limited. The purposes of the more perfect union to be established by and pursuant to the Constitution—as set forth in the preamble—barely glance at the foreign relations of the new republic to be. The Constitution enumerates, and allocates to the political branches, some foreign affairs powers—commerce with foreign nations, war, treaties—but many powers that are indisputably foreign affairs powers (and were surely intended for the federal government and denied to the states) are not mentioned. Congress shall have the power to declare war, but there is no mention of the power to make peace. The President and Senate make treaties, but nothing is said of the undoubted power to break, terminate, or suspend a treaty. Who can "make foreign policy" in respects other than war, treaties, commerce? There is nothing, surely nothing explicit, about recognizing states or governments, about gathering intelligence and engaging in other covert activities, including "dirty tricks"; about declaring a Monroe Doctrine or a Truman Doctrine or a Nixon Doctrine or a Reagan Doctrine. There is nothing about international agreements of the United States that are not treaties; nothing about protecting United States citizens and rescuing United States hostages. There is nothing, surely nothing explicit, about the mass of decisions and actions that are the stuff of the daily relations of the United States with other countries. Neither specific clauses nor any general grant allocates authority to deploy and use military force short of going to war. There is certainly nothing about power to launch a nuclear attack, whether as a first or a second strike.

Some have suggested that the Constitution contains implicit or hidden allocations of power—in broad conceptions of the power of Congress to regulate commerce with foreign nations or to make laws necessary and proper for Congress to carry out its war powers or other powers; or in the President's "executive power" or in the Commander in Chief clause. But every argument for extrapolation of authority for Congress from one of its expressed powers is countered by an argument for inferring power for the President from one of his powers. For a contentious example, does the power to decide whether United States forces shall be deployed abroad lie with Congress under its war power, or with the Commander in Chief?

It was doubtless the meagerness of detailed prescription that led the Supreme Court some fifty years ago, in the *Curtiss-Wright* case, to conclude that as regards foreign affairs the federal government is not one of enumerated powers only; the United States has all the powers inherent in nationhood and national sovereignty, whether or not such powers are mentioned in the Constitution.[3] But if the framers provided no guidance as to where to find the powers of the federal government in international matters, of course they provided no guidance as to how such unenumerated federal authority is allocated between Congress and the President. The Court in *Curtiss-Wright* did not address that question, nor does that constitutional essay give any guidance as to the scope of the few foreign affairs powers that *are* enumerated and are explicitly allocated to one branch or the other.

Earlier "interpretivists"* might have insisted that there can be no "missing powers" and that, however hidden, they must be sought in text and context and the purpose and intent of the framers. But that prescription is not easily followed. The longevity of the Constitution has been attributed in substantial part to its prescient ambiguities. I have mentioned the uncertainty of locating the power to deploy troops for purposes short of war. There are many other such constitutional puzzles. For example, is the power to make peace to be found in the power of Congress to declare war or, since wars are commonly terminated and peace established by treaty, in the power of the President (with the advice and consent of the Senate) to make treaties? Is the power to terminate a treaty implied in the power to make it? If so,

---

* Recent controversy has pitted those who insist that constitutional principle can be legitimately derived only by interpretation of the constitutional text as against those who argue for looking beyond text to other sources and other values (see p. 73 below).

does the power to terminate a treaty—like the power to make it—require Senate advice and consent? What does interpretivism tell us as to whether there is an "executive privilege" to withhold information from Congress or a presidential right to impound and not spend funds appropriated by Congress? Are diplomatic relations, covert activities, and other aspects of foreign relations, subject to control by Congress under its power "to regulate commerce with foreign nations" or under its war power, or are they, as argued early, exclusively within the executive power of the President? Is the War Powers Resolution of 1973 (see p. 30) within the constitutional powers of Congress, as Congresses have asserted and Presidents have denied? Did President Reagan have authority to send troops to Lebanon or Grenada or to bomb Libya? Could the President, some unthinkable day, on his own authority, convert conventional war to nuclear war by "first use," retaliate against an enemy that had dropped nuclear bombs on an ally of the United States, or initiate a nuclear "first strike" to preempt an anticipated attack or for other reasons of perceived national interest?

[handwritten marginalia: Once again with the prescience, although least of it's not bad as not nuclear warfare.]

■ It has been suggested that large issues of constitutional principle or power should be decided not by pedantic parsing of particular phrases of constitutional text, but by looking to context and structure, to "grand design." Alas, for our purposes the text reveals no unambiguous grand design.* It has been suggested that what is not clear from the Constitution should be determined by the intent of the framers; alas, there is no compelling evidence of the intent of the framers, either as to the import of particular phrases as to grand design or as to many of the specific issues that agitate our constitutional universe.

Alexander Hamilton early set forth an executive view of the grand design of the Constitution for the conduct of foreign relations. In support of his argument that President Washington had authority to declare the neutrality of the United States in the war between England and France, Hamilton (writing as Pacificus) read the executive power clause in Article II of the Constitution as a grant to the President of all

---

*There is a presidential version of the grand design and a very different congressional view of the grand design. Were there a clear "grand design" it might be invoked to supply what is not determined by specific provisions; no theory of constitutional interpretation would warrant resort to grand design to contradict a clear provision in the text or its most plausible interpretation. For our purposes; there is no unambiguous grand design, and what we encounter are alternative views: the presidential version of grand design and Congress's version.

executive power and insisted that executive power included the control of foreign relations. For Hamilton, then, responsibilities and powers of foreign affairs lay with the President, except as expressly modified in the Constitution. The Constitution, we know, granted some foreign affairs powers exclusively to Congress, i.e., the power to enact laws regulating commerce with foreign nations, to appropriate funds, and to declare war. The Constitution also expressly imposed other limitations on the President's "monopoly" in foreign affairs when it made his power to make treaties or to appoint officers subject to Senate advice and consent. With those explicit exceptions, however, the President controls the conduct of foreign relations as part of the grant of executive power.*

Equally eminent "framers," however, rejected Hamilton's reading of the executive power clause and therefore his view of the design of the Constitution. James Madison (Helvidius), with encouragement from Thomas Jefferson, reacted sharply against Hamilton's view of large executive power. For Madison, the executive power clause was not a "grant in bulk of all conceivable executive power"[4] but only a heading for what follows. The President has only the powers expressly given to him, the power to make treaties and appointments (with the Senate), and those implied in his designation as Commander in Chief, and these are not to be extravagantly construed. The rest belongs to Congress.

The Hamilton-Madison debate over the meaning of the executive power clause was essentially an argument as to the grand design intended by the framers.† The intent of the framers is reflected in what they did, their deliberations, their writings, but they were not always

---

*John Marshall also contributed to the executive view of the grand design of the Constitution. In 1800, as a member of the House of Representatives, he supported the power of the President to extradite an individual pursuant to treaty. Marshall declared that the President was the "sole organ of the nation in its external relations and its sole representative with foreign nations." Marshall made this statement in the House of Representatives to justify an extradition to Great Britain. *Annals of Cong.* 10:613, reprinted in 5 Wheat. Apendix note 1, at 26 (U.S. 1820). The Supreme Court quotes that with approval in the *Curtiss-Wright* case, p. 29.

† A strong case for large congressional power in foreign affairs could be made by not-implausible interpretations of text. Congress has the power "to regulate Commerce with foreign Nations," and — as John Marshall told us early and the Supreme Court has now firmly established—commerce is not merely trade, but intercourse, all forms of intercourse. It is not excluded that, for the framers, Congress was to have power to regulate intercourse with foreign nations, not merely by enacting laws on tariffs and trade but by determining national foreign policy generally, just as, under its war power, Congress can establish national policy as to war and peace. Indeed, the War Power itself might support congressional power to determine foreign policy since, plausibly, all foreign policy is sufficiently related to war and peace so that its regulation is necessary and proper for carrying out congressional war powers. On this view Congress need not deny that the President is "sole organ," but he is the organ of communication and the sole representative to the world; the foreign policy to be communicated and represented is for Congress to determine.

certain of or agreed on their views and not wholly explicit or candid as to what they were doing.* That intent, I think, was clear in some respects, but less than certain in others.

The Convention of 1787 created a new government and a new form of government. The framers held general principles of "republicanism" —of popular sovereignty and representative government—but they were committed to no precise formula for realizing those principles and they copied no ideal model. They drew on British precedents and on their own colonial past as developed in their state constitutions, but they clearly rejected other elements in their history. They were committed to three branches of government, to "separation of powers" as a principle of good government, and to checks and balances to prevent concentration of power, but had no firm idea as to the exact division between executive and legislature. They began with a legislature, growing out of the Continental Congress, but they were committed to limited government and to individual rights and therefore rejected the great achievement of England's "Glorious Revolution," parliamentary supremacy. Within the new government the role of Congress was primary; there is no indication of an intent to deny *any* legislative or policy-making power to Congress. But the framers' intent as to the presidency is unclear. The office was a new one, and they were divided and uncertain about it. They recognized the need for a single executive to carry out executive functions, but this executive was not to be an elected monarch with power to create policy on his own authority. They wanted an institution capable of initiative and planning, therefore a single executive and a single, civilian Commander in Chief. But they had no fixed idea as to which functions were executive or how many executive functions should go to the new President and how many should stay with Congress (as under the Articles of Confederation) or which functions might be divided between them. They also feared tyranny, whether of a King or President or the tyranny of a majority represented in Congress. And what emerged from the Convention was in some respects the result of compromise and was sometimes purposefully ambiguous; much was left to the future.

There is much to support Madison's view of the framers' grand design. Under the Articles of Confederation, Congress had all—both "legislative" and "executive" authority. Experience had shown the de-

---

*Observers may have noticed that there has been little invocation of original intent in foreign affairs, surely not by the most vocal recent supporters of original intent in the executive branch.

sirability of a single executive and a single commander-in-chief, and therefore the framers created a new office for those purposes. For the rest, the framers left much where they found it under the Articles. In the Constitution, Congress comes first. The framers gave Congress "all legislative powers" of the federal government; the President was to exercise "the executive Power." That division of authority and function was to apply generally, without apparent distinction or exception for what we have come to call foreign affairs. In regard to foreign, as to domestic, affairs (our characterizations, not the Constitution's), Congress was to legislate and the President was to take care that the laws be faithfully executed.* Congress would lay taxes to provide for the common defense and general welfare of the United States, whether in domestic or foreign respects, and "no Money shall be drawn from the Treasury [whether for foreign or domestic needs] but in Consequence of Appropriations made by Law." Under the executive power the President would appoint officials with the advice and consent of the Senate, whether an attorney general or other officials in charge of domestic matters or a secretary of state for foreign affairs or an ambassador to a foreign nation.

The division between recommending legislation and enacting it, between passing laws and executing them, between appropriating money and spending it, applies in foreign as in domestic affairs.† In foreign affairs, however, that division does not exhaust the constitutional authority of the federal government. The Constitution itself confers and

*The evidence is strong that on the whole the framers intended to build as much as possible on what they had. Even when change was made it was not trumpeted. The framers of 1787 seem to have been reluctant to admit that they were making radical changes. In the Constitution they drafted they did not announce that they were creating a new government. The phrase "The Government of the United States" is buried in one place, in the "necessary and proper" clause. The framers retained appellations that were singularly inappropriate to the new dispensation. *Congress* was appropriate for the Continental Congress; it was hardly the obvious name for a legislature. *President* was new but was hardly the title to describe a head of state, today the most powerful in the world. (What does he preside over?) Even the name of the country remained the same: *the United States*. What sort of name is that for a country? It sounds like the "United Nations" — states more or less united — a noun with an adjective, a description more or less accurate, perhaps only an aspiration or a commitment to unity.

†Congressional supporters have sometimes claimed that constitutional uncertainties are to be resolved, and omissions supplied, by applying the principle of division between legislative and executive power: Congress makes foreign policy (our term, not a constitutional conception), and the President executes congressional policy and conducts foreign relations in accordance with that policy. But in foreign affairs the President does not merely execute what Congress prescribes. The President makes foreign policy—and even legislates, makes law—when he makes a treaty (with the consent of the Senate). He makes foreign policy when he establishes diplomatic relations, say by appointing an ambassador to the People's Republic of China and terminating such relations with Taiwan. What is more, the distinction between making foreign policy and conducting foreign relations is essentially empty: the President makes foreign policy by conducting foreign relations, by the way he conducts them and the content and tone he gives them.

allocates important powers that do not conform to the division between making and executing law. Congress was given the power to decide for war or peace—not a legislative act as commonly understood, then or now. On the other hand, the President was given the power to make treaties, and treaties were to be the law of the land. But there is more to foreign affairs than laws and expenditures, treaties and war, and neither specific grants of the Constitution nor any clear general grants of authority address the mass of decisions and actions that are the stuff of daily international relations; neither specific clauses nor general grants clearly allocate authority to determine the uses of force that are not war.

In principle, the framers divided legislative from executive power, but Hamilton was not alone in stressing that the conduct of foreign relations was "executive altogether."[5] The presidency was to have some foreign affairs powers that under the Articles of Confederation had been exercised by Congress. But the framers did not make the President a republican, elected facsimile of the King of England, with republican-royal powers and republican-royal prerogatives. Above all, the President was not to have the King's power to go to war; that power was given to Congress. The President was entrusted with the "royal" power to make treaties, but subject to the advice and consent of the Senate, indeed, of an extraordinary majority, two-thirds of the Senators present. Another presidential foreign affairs function was not designated a power, but seems rather an assignment: the President "shall receive foreign ambassadors."

During the ensuing two hundred years, Presidents have prominently and frequently claimed large powers by virtue of their constitutional designation as Commander in Chief. There is little support for such claims in text or original intent. Strictly, "the President shall be Commander in Chief of the Army and Navy" is a designation, or assignment, not a grant of power (though some powers may be necessarily implied in the function). Having learned a lesson in the Revolutionary War, the framers determined that there should be a single, civilian Commander in Chief, rather than command by Congress or congressional committee. The evidence is that in the framers' contemplation, the armed forces would be under the command of the President but at the disposition of Congress. Principally, the President would command the forces in wars declared by Congress. As an exception, the framers agreed to leave to the executive "the power to repel sudden attacks":[6]

authorization by Congress might not be possible to obtain promptly, or at all, and could be assumed. There is no evidence that the Framers contemplated any significant independent role — or authority — for the President as Commander in Chief when there was no war. Congress would decide whether "to raise and support Armies" or "to provide and maintain a Navy" and would "make rules for the Government and Regulation" of such forces; it was Congress that would even "provide for calling forth the Militia." There was to be no standing army for the President to command in time of peace and no army or navy at all unless Congress raised or provided it. The President's designation as Commander in Chief, then, appears to have implied no substantive authority to use the armed forces, whether for war (unless the United States were suddenly attacked) or for peacetime purposes, except as Congress directed.

No doubt, there was more that the framers did not articulate, and much they did not anticipate, perhaps some things they purposely did not provide for. The framers, I am persuaded, had a reasonably clear idea of the powers they were conferring upon Congress: in general, they saw Congress as the principal "policy-making" (our term, not theirs) organ in foreign as in domestic affairs, and in their conception Congress was to dominate the political process. They had a much less clear view about the new office they were projecting, the presidency. They allocated to the President particular functions, and they did perhaps intend that he should have executive powers other than those specified, but these did not add up to a comprehensive, coherent conception of his office or of the division of authority between Congress and President; surely there was no consensus about it among the framers. Except as they expressly provided, many of the framers were content, I suspect, to leave the office undefined in the good hands of the man all expected would be the first President. George Washington would shape the office.

■ The life of the Constitution, too, has not been logic or textual hermeneutics, but experience, and constitutional history has supplied answers to some of the questions that constitutional text and "original intent" left unanswered. In my view, Madison had the better of the argument from text, design, and intent, but history has tilted toward Hamilton. George Washington did indeed begin to shape the office, along Hamiltonian lines, not on principle or in accordance with plan or grand design, but in response to opportunity and perceived needs. The President's place in the configuration of government combined with the character of foreign relations to shape the modern presidency, as well as to launch it on the paths of uncertainty and controversy.

The major developments in the conception and scope of the presidential office concerned matters that were not on the face of the Constitution, but resulted from what the Constitution provided. The President appointed ambassadors; they were his ambassadors, and they received instructions from him and reported to him. They did so in secret, the way of diplomacy even in the eighteenth century. Through his ambassadors the President communicated with other governments as seemed appropriate to him. The President told Congress what his judgment and his sense of diplomatic and constitutional propriety required.

Foreign policy, then as now, consisted of much more than making treaties or legislating tariffs. Then as now, the conduct of foreign relations was a day-to-day process, continuous and informal. Unlike Congress, dispersed during most of our early history in the distances of the country, the presidency was always "in session." Unlike Congress, which can act only formally, by statute or resolution (and therefore in effect only publicly and sometimes dramatically), the President can act quickly and informally, often discreetly or secretly: only President Washington could decide to send Citizen Genêt home when he abused his post as Minister of France; only Washington could effectively pursue the deliberations and negotiations that led to a decision to proclaim neutrality in the wars between England and France. In many circumstances, unless the President acted, the United States could not act at all. Major agreements were made as treaties with the consent of the Senate, but the practice of the President acting alone to make informal agreements (and some formal ones) were inevitable and began early.

From the beginning, the President, as "sole organ" of communication, as representative to the world, was the eyes, ears, and voice of the United States. Slowly, he became its nerve center, too. He began to "make policy." He declared neutrality in the wars between England and France; he decided that we would purchase Louisiana and acquire Florida; he announced the Monroe Doctrine. But the President also became the sturdy arms of the United States. Congress provided and maintained a small navy and occasionally raised and supported a modest army; as the Constitution provided, the President was their commander. In response to events, Presidents asserted authority to use those forces: early, Jefferson ordered the navy to defend United States vessels against the "Barbary pirates."

As our Presidents' "foreign relations power" took root and grew, they found themselves wearing two hats. In limited, uncertain steps the President as Commander in Chief began to carry out what the President as foreign affairs executive determined. In time, precedents accumulated and Presidents gained confidence and claimed more authority. Beginning early and continuing to this day, in several hundred instances of varying scope and significance, Presidents have deployed the armed forces of the United States for foreign policy purposes determined by the President on his own authority.

Congress contributed to the steady growth of presidential power. Congress early recognized and confirmed the President's control of day-to-day foreign intercourse, and the resulting monopoly of information and experience promoted presidential claims of expertise and a congressional sense of inadequacy. Congress generally acquiesced even in the President's deployments of forces, and the Senate in his executive agreements. Later, a growing practice of informal consultations between the President and congressional leaders disarmed them as well as members of Congress generally and helped confirm presidential authority to act without formal congressional participation. Often Congress quickly ratified or confirmed what the President had already done, such as, in contemporary times, the decision in 1950 to fight in Korea.* And repeatedly Congress delegated its own huge powers to the President in broad terms so that he could later claim to have acted under the authority of Congress as well as his own, as in the Tonkin Gulf Resolution of 1964, which in effect legitimated the Vietnam War. What Presidents have done with congressional acquiescence, or even by congressional delegation, has come to be claimed and seen as presidential power.

In our legalist-constitutionalist political culture, practice was early undergirded by doctrine. Hamilton's argument for large executive power, although not adopted by the Supreme Court[7] or accepted by Congress, has remained a staple of presidential claims. John Marshall's

---

*Congress appropriated money for the conduct of the war without questioning the President's authority.

characterization of the presidency (see p. 22 above) was expressly approved by the Supreme Court in *Curtiss-Wright* (1936), where the Court referred to "the very delicate, plenary and exclusive power of the President as the sole organ of the federal government in the field of international relations."[8] Later Presidents blended Hamilton's "executive power" and Marshall's "sole organ" and built on them. In our century Theodore Roosevelt claimed to be the "steward of the people" and insisted that his "executive power was limited only by specific restrictions and prohibitions appearing in the Constitution or imposed by the Congress under its Constitutional powers."[9] Franklin Roosevelt —in time of war—also claimed authority from "the people" and even threatened to repeal an act of Congress (or to treat it as repealed).[10] More recent Presidents have avoided having to justify, and inviting reaction to, extravagant conceptions of the presidential office by simply asserting far-reaching authority "under the Constitution and the laws of the United States." The constitutional pretensions of the Roosevelts have not been invoked or imitated recently, but it has sometimes been asserted, and often assumed, that the President himself can determine the foreign policy of the United States, can communicate that policy as "sole organ," can implement it as "the executive," and can enforce it as Commander in Chief.

■ Regardless of Madisonian arguments, history has given the President large powers as executive in foreign affairs and as Commander in Chief of the armed forces. History, it should be clear, has not given the President what the Constitution clearly gave to Congress alone: the President cannot enact laws in the United States; he cannot wage war (unless the United States is attacked); he cannot spend money unless Congress has authorized and appropriated it.

Even if history has given the President large powers, it has not necessarily reduced congressional authority. In Justice Jackson's terms, what history seems to have given the President is concurrent authority in a twilight zone in which the President can act when Congress is silent. Concurrent power may inspire a race for initiative, and in general the initiative is with the President, but the claims of Congress in the twilight zone are strong, and when Congress acts, its claims for supremacy are strong. In his essay on presidential authority, Justice Jackson wrote: "When the President takes measures incompatible with the expressed or implied will of Congress, his power is at its lowest ebb, for then he can rely only upon his own constitutional powers minus any constitutional powers of Congress over the matter."[11]

It has been commonly accepted by students of the Constitution, if not always by Presidents, that except in a small zone of exclusive presidential authority, Congress acting under its broad powers can prohibit or regulate what the President does and the President (and all the President's men) may not flout congressional directives. Until recently, in fact, Presidents had rarely asserted power to act when Congress has directed them not to or to disregard conditions imposed by Congress on their actions.

In recent years, the focus of debate has moved. Congress has become more concerned and more active, imposing limitations on the executive where Presidents had come to think of themselves as essentially autonomous and having the final word: Congress has regulated the executive in regard to the use of force, "covert activities," the sale of arms to terrorist states, and foreign aid to governments guilty of gross violations of human rights. Presidents have resisted. Presidential authority to act when Congress has not is assumed; now it is claimed that presidential authority is supreme to or even exclusive of Congress. The issue is no longer the President's power, but the power of Congress. Congress now is charged with "congressional activism," with being an "imperial Congress," implying that congressional regulation such as that indicated is improper, usurping, and unconstitutional.

In the principal source and context of continuing controversy, the War Powers Resolution of 1973, Congress declared that the President's constitutional power to introduce United States forces into hostilities, or into situations where imminent involvement in hostilities in clearly indicated, is strictly limited, and Congress proceeded to regulate such uses of force stringently.[12] President Nixon vetoed the resolution, asserting that it was "clearly unconstitutional."[13] The veto message did not say why the resolution was beyond the powers of Congress or which presidential powers it violated. Succeeding Presidents have reiterated that the resolution was unconstitutional but have given no clearer reason why.

Mr. Nixon supported the conclusion that the War Powers Resolution was unconstitutional by the statement that the resolution attempted "to take away . . . authorities which the President has properly exercised under the Constitution for almost 200 years." But the President exercised those "authorities" during those 200 years when Congress was silent. The President acted, and Congress did not resist. But the President did not act contrary to congressional legislation. History supports few limitations on the power of Congress in foreign affairs other than the Bill of Rights, and history gives no support for any presidential authority to flout congressional legislation in the matters we are addressing. The President would have to find foreign affairs and Commander in Chief powers that give the President power exclusive of Congress, and there is little basis for that in text, original intent, or history.

Presidential foreign affairs powers and powers as Commander in Chief, exclusive of Congress and not subject to its control, have no basis in Alexander Hamilton or in John Marshall. In the early controversies the issue was whether the President had authority to act on his own initiative, without authorization from Congress. The issue was the constitutional authority of the President, not the authority of Congress. There was little occasion to question the constitutionality of any congressional initiative. There was no claim by the executive of authority to act contrary to an act of Congress. Hamilton argued for the power of the President to act when Congress was silent, indeed to act so as to preserve the situation so that Congress could act later; there is nothing in Hamilton to suggest that the President can flout congressional legislation or that the expressed powers of Congress must be narrowly construed so as to leave more for the President's exclusive discretion. For Marshall, the President is the sole organ of the United States for communication and representation. Marshall did not claim sole Presidential authority to determine or control the policies that are to be communicated or represented. Marshall said nothing, implied nothing, about limitations on Congress other than as regards communication and representation to other governments.

If the President presses his resistance, Congress can usually prevail, in constitutional principle and in governmental practice, if only because it holds the purse strings. The significance of Congress's power of the purse should not be misconceived. Under the Constitution the President cannot spend a dollar unless Congress has authorized and appropriated the money. But where the President has independent constitutional authority to act, Congress, I believe, is constitutionally bound to implement his actions, notably by appropriating the necessary funds; for example, Congress may not properly refuse to appropriate funds, as reasonably necessary, to pay for an embassy to a government the President has recognized. But when Congress is of the view that the President is acting outside his constitutional authority, it may challenge that action and may refuse to appropriate funds to implement it. Similarly, when Congress reasonably believes that the President's authority to act is not exclusive but subject to regulation by Congress, it may prohibit or limit the President's activity directly by legislation or indirectly by denying him funds. The President has no constitutional power, in any circumstances, to expend funds or transfer United States property contrary to Congressional directions. When Congress and the President do not agree, when Congress thinks the President is not acting within his constitutional authority and the President thinks he is, when Congress regulates and the President resists regulation and denies Congress's power to regulate, Congress can prevail through the power of the purse. But the President would accuse Congress of violating its constitutional oath by keeping him from carrying out his constitutional oath. There lies the field of constitutional confrontation under clouds ever threatening constitutional crisis.

Text, context, design, intent and history have combined to give us the constitutional jurisprudence we have today.

- The President has sole and exclusive authority over diplomacy and the diplomatic process, the recognition of states and governments, the maintenance of diplomatic relations, the conduct of negotiations, the gathering of intelligence. These are not subject to congressional interference, and Congress is obligated to support the President with necessary and proper laws and money. In our day, for example, President Carter determined, over significant congressional opposition, to recognize the mainland Chinese regime and to terminate recognition, diplomatic relations, and the defense treaty with the regime in Taiwan. He settled the Iran hostage crisis by executive agreement.* The President has determined the intelligence-gathering activities of the intelligence agencies, and Congress has not attempted to interfere.
- That which requires the force of law in the United States and that which requires public funds need formal resolution or

*The Supreme Court upheld this agreement (*Dames & Moore v. Regan*, 453 U.S. 654 (1981), finding that Congress had long acquiesced in and accepted the President's authority to settle international claims by executive agreement.

legislation and appropriation by Congress. As to these, the President can recommend measures for congressional consideration, but they cannot be made effective without legislation and appropriation by Congress. Congress makes all laws, including tariffs, and decides all expenditures. Congress determines foreign assistance—to which countries, in what amounts. The President sometimes promises financial or military aid, but he and the proposed recipients are aware that Congress will determine whether that promise will be kept, within what limits, and on what terms and conditions. Congress can delegate some of that power to the President, subject to clear guidelines.

■ The decision to take the country into war is for Congress. Whether Congress may delegate that war power is doubtful. The President may respond to an attack on the United States. The President may deploy forces for foreign policy purposes, but he may not, without congressional authorization, engage them in hostilities that amount to war, or put them where they court war.

■ The President plans military policy and strategy, but only Congress can appropriate funds for research and development of weapons and for the acquisition of weapons and their deployment. When Congress appropriates funds for particular weapons, it can be seen as approving or acquiescing in the strategy that those weapons imply. Congress has not yet worked out the proper balance between its responsibility to legislate and to provide for the common defense and its need to delegate and its desire to maintain "oversight," but under the Constitution it is for Congress to decide. There are recurrent demands that Congress examine untested assumptions about the President's authority to act in unthinkable ways in unthinkable circumstances—if nuclear deterrence fails. And in certain scenarios—for unspeakable contingencies when there is no President—there are grave issues of presidential succession which surely are not for the President to decide and which Congress perhaps may not properly leave to him to decide.

■ The President can make the judgments and initiate the stream of informal decisions and actions that constitute foreign policy and foreign relations, including perhaps covert activities and even some uses of the armed forces for foreign policy purposes short of war. But those activities are subject to control by Congress, whether by legislation or by control of appropriations. If Congress acts, the President shall take care that its laws be faithfully executed. Congress has exercised authority to regulate and oversee "covert activities" (for purposes other than gathering intelligence); in the Iran-Contra mess, there apparently were gross violations of the law, but no serious challenge to the constitutionality of those laws. Some Presidents have not liked congressional human rights policies, whether sanctions against South Africa on account of apartheid or restrictions on aid to other gross violators of human rights in Latin America, but no President has seriously questioned the constitutional authority of Congress to determine the policy.

My thumbnail summation, I stress, still leaves substantial areas of uncertainty: What are the reaches of the President's exclusive domain? What is "law," which only Congress can make? What is "war," which only Congress can make? What can Congress delegate to the President? The major constitutional issues in our day involve the efforts of an "activist" Congress to regulate what Presidents have come to think of as within their powers and which Congress had not previously attempted to regulate—war powers, covert activities, certain executive agreements. There are also general issues between President and Congress that have important applications in foreign affairs, notably claims of executive privilege that Congress challenges and congressional strings attached to laws or appropriations that Presidents resent and sometimes resist.

■ I have emphasized constitutional uncertainties and the conflicts they engender. Students of constitutional politics might suggest that the issues that agitate congressional-presidential relations after two hundred years reflect more than the uncertainties of the twilight zone and of constitutional interpretation. Some tensions between Congress and the President are the inevitable, intended (and perhaps desirable) consequences of the separation of powers—frictions and inefficiencies that separation engenders, failures in the cooperation that national interest may sometimes demand but that is not easy to achieve.* Some tensions in constitutional politics, such as those reflected in the Iran-Contra shame, derive at bottom not from constitutional uncertainties but from unhappiness with what the Constitution apparently prescribes. Presidents in particular, I think, often see the constitutional blueprint as being out of date for the country we have become, in the world in which we live: United States interests in the nuclear age, Presidents insist, require that there be few restraints on presidential initiative in foreign affairs and little congressional control or oversight.

For many, on the other hand, the Constitution as history has shaped it is essentially satisfactory. The Constitution intended that decisions implicating national trade policy, national spending, defense spending, war and peace, be made by Congress. History has not shown that allocation of authority to have been mistaken. Text has proven sufficiently porous or flexible, experience has provided varied precedents, institutions have been malleable, arrangements and procedures not beyond adaptation by ingenuity. What is needed, they would suggest, is not greater freedom for presidential initiative, but more effective congressional scrutiny and restraints on the executive. At least, there must be congressional participation in and responsibility for legislation, spending, and war policy and, where delegation is necessary or desirable, congressional guidance for executive initiative.

We are not likely to amend the Constitution to redistribute the authority allocated by the framers to the different political branches or to resolve what they did not anticipate or did not make clear beyond dispute. Authority can be effectively redistributed by self-restraint, by delegation, and by cooperation. Uncertainties can be resolved by constitutional construction, taking account of all that is proper stuff for constitutional interpretation—text, context and grand design, framers' intent, history, contemporary need.

In constitutional construction, as well as in considering arrangements for delegation and interbranch cooperation, it is time we paid more attention to the ideology that animates our polity. The framers

---

*Justice Brandeis wrote that "the doctrine of the separation of powers was adopted by the Convention of 1787, not to promote efficiency but to preclude the exercise of arbitrary power. The purpose was, not to avoid friction, but, by means of the inevitable friction incident to the distribution of the governmental powers among three departments, to save the people from autocracy" (Myers v. United States, 272 U.S. 52, 293 (1926) (Brandeis, J., dissenting).

made their division of authority in foreign affairs on the basis of their commitment to constitutionalism and of their concerns to achieve government in the public interest as effective as is consistent with safeguards against concentration of power and tyranny. The system we have developed, providing for presidential initiative guided by Congress and subject to congressional brakes, responds also to the special character of American democracy. Constitutionalism and democracy, I suggest, should be invoked to resolve disputes and to guide the branches in the exercise of their allotted authority.

Students of constitutional law are reminded repeatedly of John Marshall's famous admonition that "We must never forget, that it is a *constitution* we are expounding."[14] For Marshall, that dictum meant something like "it is a Constitution, not a bill of lading," a special case of a general principle of interpretation: a legal document should be construed in accordance with its character and purpose. In that spirit, this dictum has suggested a "large" construction of text and of particular terms; it has suggested not "parsing" but attention to "grand design." Marshall's dictum, I think, means also that we must remember that our Constitution is "a constitution" and establishes "constitutionalism." Constitutionalism implies a commitment to respect the written social contract, so far as it is clear. Constitutionalism implies that the Constitution should be construed so as to maintain the commitment to limited government, to reject "imperial powers" not subject to balance and control.

Constitutionalism implies limited government. For our subject, that means that the Constitution should be expounded so that there can be no extraconstitutional government, that, in principle and in effect, no activity of government is exempt from constitutional restraints, not even foreign affairs: government cannot exercise unlimited authority in any large area—not even in foreign affairs. We have remained committed to limited government, if no longer from a priori commitment to the limited purposes of government then from abiding commitment to individual rights. We continue to revere checks and balances and some separation of powers, perhaps from habit or piety, perhaps from an underlying commitment to avoiding concentration of power. For us, as for the framers, no branch of government has authority that is so large as to be essentially undefined and uncircumscribed, that is "plenary," that is not checked, not balanced, not even the President, not even in foreign affairs. Therefore, there is little presidential author-

ity that is not subject to scrutiny and control by Congress.* Constitutionalism is not mesmerized by invocations of efficiency, by extravagant
claims of "necessity" (even when clothed in irresistible formulae, such
as "national security," "national interest," or *raison d'état*).
American constitutionalism is also committed to the sovereignty of
the people. Two hundred years ago, "the people" was limited in fact if
not in principle; the framers of the Constitution were republicans, not
democrats, or at least more republicans than democrats. Neither Congress nor the President was authentically representative. Representatives to the House of Representatives were elected by a small percentage of the population. The Senate was not elected at all and represented
states, not people. The President was chosen by electors.

Constitutional amendment and new constitutional interpretations, I
have noted, have made us a democracy. It is not inappropriate, I
suggest, to assimilate that development in our constitutional history
and to invoke our democracy to guide construction of the Constitution, not least the authority of the now-democratic branches. Such
constitutional development, more than eighteenth-century definitions
of executive and legislative power, should determine the divisions of
constitutional authority in foreign affairs in the third century.

In general, and prima facie, a constitution that ordains constitutional democracy, I conclude, should be expounded so that—in foreign affairs as elsewhere—the institutions and procedures it establishes
will promote maximum attention to the will of the people and the
consent of all the governed; the largest participation by the people and
the most authentic representation of them; more rather than less responsiveness, responsibility, accountability, and, therefore, broad-rather
than narrow-based decision making; the most open government most
likely to lead to wise policy responding to the people's values.

Of course, ours is a unique, dual democracy. The President is now
also effectively elected by the people. Both Congress and the President
are representative; both are responsible, both accountable. But their
representative character and their accountability are different, and the
differences should reflect and be reflected in their authority. In domestic affairs, both are representative, but the President proposes and
Congress disposes and legislates; then the President executes and Congress oversees and reexamines its legislation. In foreign affairs, the

---

*Constitutionalism requires also that no part of governance be exempt from judicial review—
not even in foreign affairs. See chapter 3.

President represents the people of the United States to the world. Congress represents the people at home, the different regions, groups, constituencies, and interests (general and special). And the representative functions of the President and Congress are different. The President leads and initiates; Congress deliberates, legislates, confirms (or rejects); Congress can also anticipate and regulate, even in foreign affairs. The presidency is confidential, classified; Congress is open and more accessible for citizen participation. Both are accountable, but the President's accountability is essentially plebiscitarian quadrennially. Congress—its members—are accountable directly, daily.

Appeals to constitutionalism and to democracy cannot change the constitutional text, the basic framework of distinct branches. We are constitutional positivists, and there has been no serious suggestion that we transform all our institutions better to reflect our new democracy. But where fairly possible, where constitutional spaces and silences require or permit, democracy, I suggest, is the best matter to fill them with. For that large twilight zone where text is silent, where original intent is uncertain, where history is at best ambiguous, the principles and the values of democracy may be determinative.

Constitutionalism-democracy in the third century, I conclude, requires that we shape our form of government accordingly, not merely because our eighteenth-century Constitution commits us to eighteenth-century notions of governmental functions, eighteenth-century ideas of "executive power," and the framers' uncertain compromises in adjusting the functions of the branches. Constitutionalism cum democracy must mean that we do things differently from those not committed to them. We act differently from those in the USSR—committed to neither constitutionalism nor democracy. We act differently even from the United Kingdom, where there is democracy, but not constitutionalism in our sense—no limited government, no checks and balances, no entrenched individual rights, no judicial review. That we have to deal with "nonconstitutional" countries does not mean that we can do so any differently than our constitutionalism and our democracy call for.

So, in foreign affairs, too, we need checks and balances. In foreign affairs, too, neither the framers not we were (are) disposed to sacrifice parliamentary supremacy to the executive—what the British had won in the "Glorious Revolution." In foreign affairs, too, we want neither an imperial President nor an imperial Congress. Our kind of constitutional democracy ought to eschew large powers in one set of hands, surely in matters of war and peace implicating the life and death of the citizens and the nation. In our dual democracy we should have congressional delegation with control and presidential initiative subject to control. We need institutions and procedures that will assure joint congressional-executive action.

Seeing the President and Congress under the aspect of democracy confirms the judgment of the framers and the national experience in surprising measure. Consider the authority to use force—the perennial and paramount constitutional issue. The Constitution gave the decision as to whether to put the country into war to Congress; the framers intended for the President only the power to defend the United States if this country were suddenly attacked. That division still seems wise and responsive to popular wishes—the basis of authentic democracy. It is not a power that Congress should delegate. Congress might decide now that in given circumstances (say, an attack on United States forces in Berlin) the United States should go to war without awaiting a formal declaration of war by Congress; if so, Congress might so provide now, authorizing the President to act in these defined circumstances but also require appropriate if less-than-formal participation by congressional agents before that action is taken. But the decision is for Congress. (Congress might also consider rewriting the War Powers Resolution accordingly.)

The original allocation of war powers by the framers resists tooready application to the decisions of nuclear defense policy and the implications of deterrence, but its underlying sense, I think, is not irrelevant there too. Should the President have authority to decide, alone, to escalate to nuclear war, to launch a first strike? Should he decide, alone, how to respond to nuclear attack? Such power is not what the framers intended or would have intended for the President; it is not, I think, what our kind of democracy requires. Commitment to total war should require the consent of the governed, not only for the general policy but for its every cost and for all those decisions that implicate the lives—and the soul—of the people. Such decisions, I think, should be for Congress to make; surely Congress must be involved in some important way. If, in some scenarios, a situation calls for instant retaliation or urgent preemptive action and there can be no formal role for Congress, it is all the more important that Congress be involved in advance planning, in determining contingent policy, as well as in the ultimate decision, by the best procedures Congress can devise.

The exercise of force in situations other than war is another, more complicated matter. The President has acquired authority to use the forces that Congress puts at his command for foreign policy purposes. But the Constitution clearly denies him the power to intitiate war and therefore must deny him authority to do what is likely to bring us into war. A line between foreign affairs and war is not easily drawn. (Clausewitz, we know, identified war as the conduct of foreign relations by particular means.) But it is a line drawn by the framers and redrawn by our history; I think it corresponds to the intimations of our dual democracy.

Surely the answer is not confrontation between President and Congress. The stakes are too high for a democratic society to tolerate either a presidential fait accompli or a congressional fiat delivered to an unwilling President. We need processes that will bring to bear wisdom as well as expertise and the authentic consent of the governed. The original constitutional plan, the lessons of our intervening history, and our kind of democracy all call for congressional involvement, with a determining voice, in making foreign policy decisions that relate to the war power.*

For the incredible excesses of the secret arms sales to Iran and the flouting of the laws of Congress as regards Nicaragua, I see no constitutional excuse. Covert activities that stir issues of war and peace or that spend the country's resources are—and ought to be—subject to control by Congress. I believe the Constitution entrusts them to Congress properly, wisely. If the President cannot persuade Congress, he must bow to its will. The Constitution is clear: "He shall take care that the laws [of Congress] be faithfully executed."

In the end, I see no need for amendment or radical reconstruction of the Constitution as regards foreign affairs in particular. The checks

*I am suggesting a distinction akin to but different from that which Congress adopted in the War Powers Resolution. The President must eschew involvement, or serious danger of involvement, in undertakings that have the character of war or threaten to involve us in the costs of war. President Carter's attempt to rescue hostages held in Iran, for example, was not designed to fight a war and was not likely to engage Iranian forces or threaten the independence or territorial integrity of Iran—the relevant test under international law. The invasion of Grenada, by contrast, whatever motivated it, sought to topple a government and occupy a territory. It was widely seen as an act of war for international purposes, and it would seem to have had the character of war for constitutional purposes. Good fortune kept deaths few on both sides, and as a result the action won popular acclaim. But would the people have supported it had it proved costly? It is not, I think, the kind of action the Constitution and our dual democracy intend to be undertaken by the President on his own authority. Again, the War Powers Resolution might be rewritten to reflect the distinctions I suggest.

and balances intended by the framers and—in my view—justified by our history, as well the effective representation, responsibility, and accountability ("democracy") required by our ideology today, can be assured under our contemporary constitutional jurisprudence, as I see it. The responsibility for maintaining them lies with both political branches, but it is ultimately in the hands of Congress. Congress can exercise that responsibility by regulation, by delegation, by oversight, or even by abstinence and acquiescence, but even abstinence and acquiescence should be knowing, intentional, purposeful. Congressional "activism" is not usurpation; it is mandatory. Only Congress can assure both checks and balances and democracy in foreign affairs.

■ We have come a long way under the constitutional blueprint that the framers ordained and established.

In the large, we are governed in the way the framers contemplated. After two hundred years of the Constitution, Congress and the presidency are transformed, but in major respects their parts in our governance are recognizably those projected by the constitutional blueprint: Congress makes laws and the President executes them; Congress levies taxes to provide for the common defense and the general welfare, and the President spends as Congress directs. In those respects, the constitutional division of authority between Congress and President is reasonably clear, indisputable, and therefore not often disputed, though both Congress and the President have sometimes tried to move or blur the line that divides their estates. In foreign as in domestic affairs, that constitutional division continues to provide the framework and context of government. In both domestic and foreign affairs, magnified presidential importance derives not from any new constitutional powers or functions granted to (or assumed by) him, but from the enlarged significance of the powers, privileges, and duties originally conferred upon him, from large delegations of power by Congress, as well as from extraconstitutional factors, notably the President's political dominance—party leadership, patronage, popular appeal—and his consequent ability to persuade, move, and sometimes compel Congress.

That which text—whether literally or liberally construed—does not determine with confidence has been supplied from other relevant sources. The life of constitutional law, too, has been experience and adaptation to new needs in a new world. Is it right that we do not hear overmuch about original intent? The framers did not anticipate, I think, how much legislation and spending would be determined by the fact that the President recommended them; that the President would become the many-headed executive branch, knowledgeable, expert, and difficult for Congress to resist or to overrule; or how much power Congress would be "compelled" or disposed to delegate to the President with only vague guidelines for its exercise. I doubt they foresaw the number and variety of agreements Presidents would claim authority to make without advice and consent of the Senate. The framers did not foresee the consequence of leaving general policies to be executed by a President who also had the command of the armed forces. I do not think they foresaw the President's claim to use the armed forces for broad foreign policy purposes determined by him. Surely they did not foresee a nuclear world and nuclear strategy that induced Congress to delegate—or abandon—its constitutional authority over the life of the nation to the President and even to unspecified persons in his command. It is not irrelevant to constitutional interpretation that Presidents, including some not particularly "imperialist" in their conceptions of office, saw fit to assert claims to constitutional authority that are not obviously granted them by the Constitution and that Congresses—never diffident about asserting the authority of the legislative branch—have acquiesced in large presidential claims. The teachings of experience, however, are sometimes ambiguous, and even after two hundred years new issues arise for the first time and old issues recur in garb and context sufficiently new to challenge earlier precedents.

The important issue, I suggest, is no longer whether the President can take initiatives or, I believe, whether Congress can regulate by law or appropriation. The issue is rather whether the President *should* take particular initiatives without congressional authorization. The courts, then, could not decide such questions even if they were prepared to abandon extravagant conceptions of what is a political question and a narrow view of what is justiciable (see chapter 3). I have suggested that we find guidance in authentic constitutional principle and our contemporary political theory. We come down, I think, to deciding— if we can—what kind of country we are and wish to be. I am disposed to state the question as: how should foreign affairs be run in a republic that has become a democracy? I have tried to make the case for dual responsibility, ultimately congressional responsibility.

The Constitution was not a perfect realization of ideals, principles, and plans, but "a mosaic of everyone's second choices." As a result, ours is a strange system, the strangest in the world. It was strange when it was conceived; it is stranger in the nuclear age. After two hundred years, it blends constitutionalism and democracy, commitment to diffused authority and individual rights with government by the governed today. It also blends different notions of democracy: a democracy represented to the world, principally by the President, and an internal democracy represented principally by Congress. It blends both constitutionalism and democracy with concern for effectiveness, but for different kinds of effectiveness at different functions. The President provides leadership and commands information, expertise, secrecy, speed, and efficiency. Congress represents the people's wider, more sober, more deliberate (more cautious) long-term values and judgments. Like it or not, the representatives of our different kinds of democracy have to work together. Constitutionalism, individual rights, and good government as well as democracy demand fewer decisions by one representative alone, for war or in peace.

2

TREATIES IN A
CONSTITUTIONAL DEMOCRACY

■

Most recent constitutional controversy has involved "war powers" and other powers of Congress and of the President that fall within a constitutional "twilight zone," which their respective authority is uncertain or their powers may be concurrent (see p. 2). I suggested that in general, presidential resistance to congressional control on constitutional grounds (as distinguished from other kinds of grounds) is not supported by the text of the Constitution, its grand design, the framers' intent, or two hundred years of history. I pleaded the claims in constitutional construction of principles of constitutionalism and of our emerged, dual, representative democracy and suggested that both constitutionalism and democracy call for arrangements that will ensure joint decision by Congress and President in major actions in foreign affairs, especially on issues of war and peace. Now I revisit the treaty power, recently a focus of controversy arising out of major arms control agreements with the Soviet Union. I inquire whether the provisions governing treaties, ordained in 1789 for an "aristocratic republic (see pp. 9–10), are appropriate to the constitutional democracy we have become.

The constitutional issues of treaty making are different from those of the twilight zone. The twilight zone is the field of tension between Congress as legislature and the President as executive and as Commander in Chief; issues in treaty making are between the President and one chamber of Congress, the Senate, acting in an executive capacity and exercising what the framers assumed to be an executive function. The twilight zone is an arena of competition for unexpressed, uncertain constitutional authority; treaty making provides principally a study of friction in the exercise of an explicit constitutional mandate to share power. But the two sets of issues, sharing a common history, reflect the same political transformations. As regards treaty making— as for the twilight zone—history has reshaped what the framers probably intended. Here too there is some unhappiness with the original dispositions and some pressure for reallocating them. Here too, I will suggest, principles of constitutionalism and democracy are relevant, both to the issues that have arisen under the existing constitutional mandate and to recurrent proposals for change.

I address principally relations between "the Treaty-Makers," the President and Senate, under Article II, section 2, where constitutional controversy has recurrently—and again recently—swirled. I consider also, briefly, the relevance of constitutionalism and democracy to our jurisprudence on treaties under the Supremacy Clause.*

CONSTITUTIONAL CONTROVERSIES ABOUT THE TREATY POWER

■ Constitutional controversies under the treaty power erupted early in our history, and during two hundred years the infinite variety of international relations and of constitutional politics have continued to generate issues. Some of the controversies reflect differences as to the meaning or implications of the constitutional text; some reflect dissatisfaction with what the text has come to mean or with how it has worked.

*Treaties appear in the Constitution principally in two contexts: the power to make treaties (Article II), and treaties as supreme law of the land (Article VI). Article I, section 10, provides that no state of the United States shall enter into any treaty. Article III provides that the judicial power of the United States shall extend also to cases arising under United States treaties.

It is unnecessary to revisit the storms generated by the Jay Treaty of 1794 or even the Treaty of Versailles, now seventy years ago; we find uncertainties and controversies in our daily papers. In 1988, the Senate denied President Reagan's power to interpret the Anti-Ballistic Missile (ABM) Treaty other than as the Senate had interpreted it when giving consent. Later the Senate in effect declared its constitutional views on that issue as a condition of its consent to the Intermediate Nuclear Force (INF) Treaty. A few years ago the Senate challenged President Carter's authority to terminate the Defense Treaty with the Republic of China (Taiwan) without the consent of Congress or at least of the Senate. Members of Congress went to court in an attempt to enjoin carrying out the Panama Canal Treaty, claiming that it was beyond the powers of the President and Senate under the Constitution.[1]

Other issues are older but recur and might yet trouble us again in the next century.* Above all, repeatedly during two hundred years, Senate and President have exchanged recriminations, the Senate accusing the President of frustrating the Senate's constitutional role, the President charging the Senate with abusing that role and embarrassing the United States in its relations with other countries. Again and again, during two hundred years, Senators have challenged the President's authority to conclude international agreements as executive agreements without Senate consent. (Senator Dole went to court to try to prevent President Carter from returning the Crown of Saint Stephen to Hungary without a treaty approved by the Senate. See p. 86.) Every year for two hundred years members of the House of Representatives have expressed resentment at their exclusion from treaty making, and there have been innumerable proposals for amending the Constitution to undo that "error" of the framers.

As for many other constitutional issues in foreign affairs, the courts have provided few answers. As a result, issues remain unresolved, constitutional processes suffer, Senate and President resort to political weapons, and constitutional relations in the United States as well as foreign relations with other governments are roiled.

For present purposes, I ask: What does the constitutional text mean, and how was it intended to work? Has history reinterpreted text or otherwise resolved issues? How has the process projected by the fram-

---

*One controversy I hope will not be resurrected: the campaign led by Senator Bricker to have the Constitution amended so as—they thought—to limit sharply the uses of the treaty power and make it impossible for the United States to adhere to international human rights covenants.

ers worked, and has it worked well enough? Do constitutional theory and democratic ideology offer guidelines or command—or commend —constitutional change, whether by formal constitutional amendment or by reinterpretation?

TEXT AND FRAMERS' INTENT

■ The constitutional provision conferring power to make treaties is brief: "[The President] shall have power, by and with the advice and consent of the Senate, to make treaties, provided two thirds of the Senators present concur." The text seems simple and clear, but even clear constitutional text is not wholly clear. Notably, we have "advice and consent," a historic phrase that has entered our daily language, but what is "advice," when and by whom is it to be given, and must it be heeded? Consent has proved clear enough, but not crystal clear: may consent be conditional, and what kinds of conditions may the Senate impose? And what is a treaty? May the President make other agreements without Senate consent?

As elsewhere in constitutional discussions of foreign affairs, here too we hear little of "original intent." But surely "original intent" has its claims, and there is some evidence as to what the framers intended. The treaty clause is an original and unique arrangement, a compromise determined by the framers. Here the framers turned their backs on Locke and Montesquieu, on British and European practice. European practice and "separation" theory saw treaty making as an executive power, but perhaps with George III on their minds, the framers were not disposed to entrust the new executive office they were creating with that much independent power by leaving treaty making to the President.

We now think of the treaty power as the President's, subject to Senate consent, but that may not have been what the framers intended. In large measure, at Philadelphia the treaty power developed separately, independently of the delegates' general conception of the new presidency-to-be.[2] The framers began with the Articles of Confederation, under which Congress—the Continental Congress, which had executive as well as legislative power—made treaties. But under the Articles, Congress needed the consent of nine states in order to make a treaty. At Philadelphia, even after it was clear that there would be an executive, the framers seemed disposed to leave treaty making to Congress or rather to one chamber of the new Congress, the Senate. Then, perhaps recalling the difficulties of negotiation and diplomacy by Congress under the Articles, the framers thought to give some role in the process to the new executive and to provide for treaty making by the Senate with the executive as its agent for negotiation. As it emerged, we know, the treaty power is listed under Article II, which begins: "The Executive power shall be vested in a President," and the power "to make treaties" is given to the President subject to Senate advice and consent. But it is not obvious that in the end the framers had decided to establish a process significantly different from what they had contemplated earlier, i.e., treaty making by the Senate with the President as the Senate's agent or perhaps joint responsibility, with the task of negotiation left to the President alone. In any event, what the framers intended, it appears, is presidential negotiation, upon advice of the Senate before negotiation, with continuing Senate advice during the process of negotiation, and, in the end, the President making the treaty to which the Senate had consented.

Note: the framers did not provide for "advice and consent" by Congress, but by the Senate alone. The Senate would not be acting as part of the legislature but in a special, executive capacity. For this role the framers selected the body that was to be the smaller, less representative, less accountable chamber of Congress. And, it appears, the framers selected the Senate for this special treaty-making role *because* it was to have those undemocratic characteristics. The Senate was also to be the special representative and guardian of state interests. Consent of two-thirds of the Senate was probably seen as not too different in effect from the consent of nine states (out of thirteen) required under the Articles.

Experience under the Treaty Power

■ History reshaped the treaty power as it reshaped other powers allocated to Congress and the President in foreign affairs. Change in the treaty process came early and continued, due to larger changes that had not been—and could not have been—anticipated. There was change in the character of the presidency and change in the character of the Senate. Political parties emerged, with their consequences for relations between executive and Senate. The United States grew, and so did its place in a changing world system. The character of United States foreign affairs changed. The role of treaties in international relations and in the foreign relations of the United States changed.

The framers had probably intended that the President and a small Senate would deliberate together, prior to and during negotiations, leading to treaties acceptable to both. The intended "advice" function atrophied and died early; in fact, advice before and during treaty negotiations hardly took off. President Washington came to the Senate with a treaty already negotiated, wanting consent, not advice; the Senate offered him advice and Washington swore never to go there again.

If Presidents had sought advice along the way, presumably there would have been an agreed United States position early, subject to modification during negotiation with the foreign country. Then Senate consent would ordinarily come easily. With the demise of advice prior to and during negotiation, the Senate considered the treaty for the first time after it was negotiated, and Senate advice appeared at the time of, and as a condition of, consent (see p. 55). The Senate used the consent requirement to "advise" the President as to the kind of treaty the Senate wanted and the kind of changes that would make the President's treaty acceptable. Often the Senate cluttered the treaty with reservations, amendments, understandings, and other conditions. Many treaties required renegotiation.

The result was a sharp bifurcation of the treaty process between the presidential stage and the Senate stage, which frustrated Presidents, annoyed foreign governments, and troubled United States foreign relations. The Senate sometimes rejected a treaty that had been carefully and painstakingly negotiated, to the embarrassment of the President and the dismay of other governments. Early in the nineteenth century foreign governments decried the United States treaty process as making it impossible to do diplomatic business with the United States. Early in our century a Secretary of State expressed doubt that an important treaty would ever again receive Senate consent. Someone described the Senate as the "grave-yard of treaties."[3] In time, the Senate became more "sophisticated": instead of rejecting a treaty, it simply shelved it (becoming not a graveyard but a place for cold storage). For a notorious contemporary example, the Genocide Convention was on the Senate shelf for thirty-seven years and was finally ratified forty-years after it was completed with the full support and participation of the United States.

The world has grown accustomed to—but not much happier with—our treaty process. Its "inefficiency" has been alleviated somewhat by some revival of the advice function. The executive now anticipates and seeks to determine the terms to which the Senate will consent. The executive branch will now consult with (i.e., seek "advice" of) Senators and Senate staff, though not formally with the whole Senate. Sometimes the President appoints a member of the Senate to the delegation negotiating an important treaty, thus providing some "advice" as to what some Senators think and what the Senate is likely to accept. But—contrary to the original intent—treaty making remains essentially a presidential power subject to Senate modification or veto. The treaty-making process continues to leave all concerned less than content—the President, the Senate, foreign governments, as well as the House of Representatives, which remains excluded from the process, and many aware citizens.

Constitutional Issues under the Treaty Power

■ The relationship between the President and Senate in treaty making became, and generally remains, adversary instead of collaborative. At best, it is often an "arms-length" relationship; sometimes it is exacerbated by antagonism and distrust. That is the notorious history of President Wilson's experience with the Versailles Treaty. In our day, SALT I and SALT II, the ABM and INF treaties, the Panama Canal Treaty, and others have not escaped friction between President and Senate.

Over two hundred years, there has been much tension between the President and Senate over treaties, but there have been few constitutional, jurisprudential issues at the heart of these tensions; rather, we have had the friction that is perhaps inevitable in the exercise of shared power by two proud, independent, separated constitutional bodies (see the famous statement by Justice Brandeis quoted on p. 66). Sometimes these tensions have been aggravated by partisan, ideological, and institutional differences. Presidents have charged the Senate with abusing its constitutional role, by delaying consent, by forcing renegotiation, by imposing improper conditions on its consent. The Senate has charged the executive with abuse of process by excluding the Senate from early planning and negotiation ("advice"), with lack of candor, concealment, and even deception. Not infrequently, Senators have declared that the President denied them access to the negotiating data and have suspected uncommunicated discussions or even secret understandings with the foreign state.

These recriminations are perhaps inevitable, systemic, built into the treaty power as it has developed. They may not be readily eliminated or easily palliated. At bottom, I stress, they are not issues of constitutional law and do not turn on constitutional construction. But in the context of a relationship susceptible to friction, small jurisprudential issues occasionally blow up into small crises, as in 1987–1988 in regard to the ABM and INF treaties. Essentially those issues reflect differences between the executive and the Senate as to constitutional implications of the treaty-making power.

■ *Implications of the Consent Requirement.* Some implications of the procedure prescribed by the Constitution are not disputed. The President can negotiate or not and can heed or disregard Senate advice if, whenever, and however given. The Senate can offer any advice; in the end, it can refuse consent for any reason or no reason; it can consent on conditions.* The President can make (bind the United States to) the treaty if the Senate has consented to it; he cannot make the treaty without Senate consent.

One implication of the constitutional requirement of Senate consent seems obvious, but it surfaced—and was confirmed—only recently in the tempest surrounding the ABM Treaty. At stake was a politically important difference between a "narrow" and a "broad" interpretation of that treaty, between a construction that would permit and one that would forbid steps toward an SDI ("Star Wars") program. But the underlying constitutional issue, though novel, was small, and the area of disagreement, though generating much heat, was comparatively narrow.

All were agreed that the President can make a treaty only if the

*Contrary to common parlance, the Senate cannot enter reservations to or amend a treaty; in effect, it refuses consent to the text as it is, while declaring that it will consent if the text is changed as indicated. This may be done ordinarily by amendment of the draft treaty by the parties (in the case of a bilateral treaty) or by reservation by the United States (in adhering to a multilateral treaty).

Senate has consented to it. Therefore, the President can make a treaty only as it was submitted to the Senate and as the Senate understood it. Generally, the Senate consents to what the text of the treaty provides, as reasonably interpreted. But if there is any ambiguity, the treaty to which the Senate consents is, inevitably, the treaty as the Senate understands it.

The Senate has often explicitly declared its understanding of the meaning of a possibly ambiguous treaty provision by an express "understanding" in its resolution of consent. If the Senate declares its understanding, the President must honor it: the treaty as so understood is the treaty to which the Senate consents. The President communicates to the other party (or parties) the Senate's understanding of the treaty as constituting the United States understanding of it, and unless the other parties reject it, that becomes the meaning of the treaty between the United States and the other parties.

In the case of the ABM Treaty, the Senate's understanding of the provision later in issue was not formally declared. But it was in fact clear (and I think not seriously disputed) that the Senate had understood the treaty to be more rather than less restrictive, less rather than more permissive. For a time, the executive branch appeared to take the position that if the Senate's understanding of a treaty was not formally declared it was of no effect and need not govern the meaning of the treaty for the United States later.* That view, I think, is mistaken: whether or not the Senate expressed an understanding, what the Senate in fact thought the treaty meant is the treaty to which it consented. The executive branch challenge to that view was untenable, and the executive may itself have abandoned it, but not without leaving severe political bruises.

The ABM confrontation was unprecedented, but it was perhaps an inevitable consequence of our unique, complex treaty process involving independent, powerful, constitutionally based institutions. The controversy involved a major security treaty, concluded after long negotiations that were heavily shrouded; the subject of the treaty—arms control generally and the particular treaty under negotiation—was

---

*There appears to have been also an issue as to the Senate's reliance on informal executive communications. The executive branch insisted, in effect, that the Senate must accept what the President formally communicates and not form any understandings on the basis of informal communications from individuals in the executive branch. There is something to be said for the view that ordinarily the Senate should not rely on views or communications of individual officials. But the Senate gives its consent to the treaty as it understands it, no matter how or from whom it obtains that understanding.

esoteric and one as to which the executive and the Senate were both ambivalent and both internally divided. Both President and Senate had been uneasy over making a commitment, both were distrustful of the USSR, and the Senate and the executive did not trust each other fully. As to the particular treaty, a later President, less than wholly sympathetic to the treaty and eager to relax its restraints, was tempted to revise an earlier President's undertakings to which the Senate had consented. But the present majority of the Senate continued to favor the treaty and resisted a new interpretation that it disfavored. Above all, the Senate was determined to vindicate its earlier consent and to preserve the integrity of its consent power.*

The controversy surrounding the interpretation of the ABM Treaty highlights larger consequences of our treaty process and of the separation of powers. In the United States, all branches of the government are bound by the text of a treaty made by the United States as the Senate understood it. Presumably, the United States must pursue that interpretation also for international purposes. But the international system—including international courts and arbitral tribunals—is not bound by the subtleties of the Unites States treaty procedure and by internal interpretations that are not expressed, adopted, and communicated to the other parties to the treaty. The international system, then, may come to an interpretation of a treaty different from the one the Senate tacitly assumed. If that happens and is established, the international interpretation of the treaty may later become the meaning within the United States as well, a consequence of the "slippage" between internal and international law in our modified "dualist" system.†

---

*The President does not have to make a treaty even after the Senate gives its consent, and the President can terminate a treaty that has been made. See p. 61. But if a treaty has been made and has not been terminated, the Senate is entitled to resist a presidential interpretation of a treaty that renders it effectively a treaty other than the one to which the Senate had consented.

The Senate was not asserting a power to interpret a treaty at a later time. Once a treaty is made, the Senate has no special authority in relation to it. The President later interprets the treaty for purposes of executing it. Congress—both houses—interprets the treaty for legislative purposes. Courts may interpret it for their purposes. The Supreme Court's interpretation of a treaty made in deciding a case or controversy is authoritative for purposes of United States law and is binding on all courts as well as on the political branches.

†"Monists" see national and international law as parts of a common legal system, with international law supreme. Dualists see national and international law as discrete legal systems, and national law determines whether to incorporate international law into national law and, if so, the place of international law in the hierarchy of the national legal system. On "monist" and "dualist" approaches to the relation of international law to national law, see, e.g., L. Henkin, R. Pugh, O. Schachter, and H. Smit, *International Law, Cases and Materials* (2d ed., St. Paul: West, 1987), pp. 140–148.

■ *Senate conditions.* As a consequence of the ABM controversy, there was constitutional confrontation in 1988 between President and Senate in the case of the INF Treaty, brought on by the Senate's power to impose conditions on its consent to a treaty. The Constitution says nothing about Senate conditions to its consent, but the development of the Senate's practice of giving consent on condition was the perhaps inevitable consequence of the demise of the Senate's advice function and the bifurcation of the treaty process between the presidential stage and the Senate stage.

Senate consent on condition developed early. Usually, the Senate has consented on condition of a change in the treaty or, in the case of a multilateral treaty, on condition that the United States adhere to the treaty subject to one or more reservations. But the Senate has learned to add other kinds of conditions that are not modifications of any international obligation under the treaty and are therefore not of importance to the other state (or states) party to the treaty. These conditions, too, are usually treaty-related, usually benign, and usually not unduly troublesome. For example, as a condition of its consent the Senate may insist that the treaty shall not be self-executing but shall require implementing legislation, sometimes even that the United States shall not ratify the treaty until implementing legislation is adopted.[4]

Important, controversial treaties in particular—in our time, notably, arms control treaties—have often evoked other "nonamending" kinds of conditions. In SALT II, for example, three kinds of "conditions" were declared, some addressed to the President, some to the USSR (the other party to the treaty), some to the world. Various conditions were imposed by the Senate in its consent to the controversial Panama Canal Treaty.*

---

*In addition to interpretive understandings discussed above and conditions to consent, the Senate has taken to attaching various "declarations" to its resolutions of consent. The Senate does not intend such declarations to be conditions upon its consent, but that seems to free the Senate to be promiscuous with its declarations and some of them are of dubious "propriety." For example, in consenting to the INF Treaty the Senate resolution appended an array of declarations of varying character. The Senate declared that because the incentive for Soviet noncompliance and the difficulties of monitoring will be great, the United States should rely primarily on its own technical means of verification. The Senate took the occasion to advise the President as to the kinds of further agreements he should negotiate. It declared its strong belief that respect for human rights and fundamental freedoms is essential to the development of friendly relations and called upon the USSR to live up to international human rights agreements, some of which the United States itself has not ratified. For the text of the Senate Resolution, see *Cong. Rec.* (daily ed., May 27, 1988), S6937:134, reprinted in *A.J.I.L.* (1988):82:810–815.

Hypothetically, the Senate might impose conditions unrelated to the treaty, e.g., that the President fire his Secretary of State or that he move the United States embassy in a certain country to a different location. Such conditions are rare and probably "improper." But could the President

Some Senate conditions are designed to enhance the power of the Senate or to constrain presidential power. For example, the Senate might decide to reserve a voice in the termination of the particular treaty, to preclude presidential termination of the treaty on his own authority as the President did in the case of the Taiwan Defense Treaty (see p. 61). Sometimes the Senate uses conditions to score in battles with the President. In consenting to the INF Treaty — following the ABM controversy — the Senate declared a principle of treaty interpretation as a constitutional principle, in the guise of a condition. The Senate resolution provides:

> That the Senate advise and consent to ratification of the Treaty . . . subject to the following —
> (a) Conditions:
> (1) Provided, that the Senate's advice and consent to ratification of the INF Treaty is subject to the condition, based on the Treaty Clauses of the Constitution, that —
> (A) the United States shall interpret the Treaty in accordance with the common understanding of the Treaty shared by the President and the Senate at the time the Senate gave its advice and consent to ratification . . .*

In my view the constitutional principle declared by the Senate is sound and its implications for treaty interpretation unexceptionable. But its title as a condition is dubious. The President, eager to make the treaty, accepted the Senate's consent subject to the Senate's "condition," but issued a statement declaring the condition to be "improper." Proper or not, such conditions are not very significant except as a salvo in President-Senate warfare in the conduct of their shared treaty power. Attaching that "condition" to a treaty does not bind future Presidents to the constitutional principle. It may not bind even the President who ratified that particular treaty, since it is not really a condition of consent but only an expression of a constitutional principle of interpretation that must stand on its merits.

Nonamending conditions sometimes reflect distrust between the United States and the other party to the treaty or Senate mistrust of the executive (or of later executives). Sometimes such conditions are blows in larger battles with the President. They reflect and inevitably

disregard them if the Senate declares that they are conditions on its consent to the treaty? Can the President treat the condition as null and the consent as unconditional?

* 134 Cong. Rec. S 6937 (daily ed. May 27, 1988).

aggravate friction in the treaty process and beyond, another consequence of our bifurcated treaty procedure.

Circumventing the Treaty Power: Executive Agreements

■ A recurrent issue between President and Senate arises from the
President's assertion of constitutional power to make some international agreements on his own authority, without consent of the Senate.
The Senate sees such agreements—sole executive agreements—as, in
principle, unconstitutional attempts to circumvent the treaty power by
excluding Senate "advice" and seeking to avoid the need for Senate
consent. There have been no recent recriminations over the issue, but
it is always in the wings as perhaps another inevitable result of the
divided treaty power.

Presidential agreements other than treaties are not mentioned in the
Constitution. But the framers clearly understood that nations make
some agreements that are not treaties,* and they could not help but
anticipate tacit, informal understandings by the President with representatives of foreign states. Early in our history, Presidents began to
make written, formal agreements on their own authority, and there
have been many thousands of such agreements made without first
obtaining the consent of the Senate or of Congress.

It is now established that the President can make some agreements
on his own authority. On the other hand, it is indisputable that there
are some agreements he cannot make without Senate consent. But
which agreements are in which category? The courts have not helped
with any general, principled guidance. They have given effect to agreements incidental to some admittedly presidential function, e.g., Franklin Roosevelt's agreement incidental to his recognition of the USSR
and claims settlements, such as the Iranian Hostages Agreement.[5]
Military armistices, such as the agreements that effectively terminated
World War I and the Korean and Vietnam wars, have been commonly
accepted as within the President's authority as Commander in Chief.

Congressional attempts to regulate executive agreements have stum-
bled over the difficulty of distinguishing agreements that the President

---

*Article I, section 10, distinguishes between treaties, which the states of the United States are
forbidden to make, and compacts or agreements with foreign powers, which states may make with
the consent of Congress.

may, should, and perhaps must conclude alone from those that should require Senate consent.* In 1969, the Senate adopted the nonbinding "National Commitments Resolution" declaring that the President could not commit the armed forces or financial resources of the United States without Senate consent or congressional approval,[6] but no President has openly accepted even that limitation. The Senate considered but did not adopt "the Clark Resolution,"[7] which sought to compel the executive branch to consult the Senate as to the method of concluding a particular agreement. To date, Congress has contended itself with requiring the executive branch to report every executive agreement made.† It is not clear that there is serious scrutiny of these agreements, but perhaps the need to report helps deter the executive from making agreements that would arouse Senate ire and invite its adverse reaction.

For the rest, we have another intractable constitutional problem. Periodically, the Senate bristles at an executive agreement, sometimes threatens to use its political weapons, both treaty- and not treaty-related, e.g., its power to hold up confirmation of the President's appointments. The Senate also has weapons in its capacity as part of the legislature, to "punish" the executive by adopting or not adopting laws or withholding appropriations.

Treaty Making in a Constitutional Democracy

■ That is the treaty power today; how does it look for the years ahead?

Unlike issues between Congress and the President in the "twilight zone," contemporary issues of treaty making do not depend on differences of interpretation of constitutional text or of original intent. What we have is chronic unhappiness with the prescribed bifurcation of the treaty power and with its implications and consequences. There appears to be an amazing acquiescence by all concerned in keeping the treaty power as it is, perhaps a reflection of a general reluctance to tamper with our constitutional institutions. If raised at all, questions about the treaty power ask how to make the existing process work

---

*The Bricker Amendment included a provision that would have limited executive agreements, and that provision might have been adopted had there been agreement as to which agreements were to be regulated.

†The original Case Act was amended to require that oral agreements be reduced to writing and transmitted, apparently to ensure that there would be no attempt to circumvent the requirement to inform Congress by making oral agreements, 1 U.S.C. § 112b. See also enforcement of Case-Zablocki Act requirements, 101 Stat. 1347, 1 U.S.C. § 112b.

better. I venture to ask first whether the constitutional procedure is consistent with our political ideology—whether the original decision of the framers to divide the treaty power continues to meet their concerns for constitutionalism and whether it responds to our commitment to democracy today (see Introduction and chapter 1). And would greater democratization of the process make it easier or more difficult for the United States to cooperate with other nations in the twenty-first century?

In fact, the treaty power—as it was conceived and as it is—may be an authentic expression of constitutionalism; surely it provides checks and balances. Giving the power to make treaties to the President, but only with Senate advice and consent, was designed and serves to limit and diffuse the treaty power and to prevent its ready and easy use. For the framers, the dominant motive of that particular form of checks and balances may have been to protect the interests of some of the states, but the result was to prevent concentration of the treaty power in the executive, as was then the practice in Europe. At the same time, the framers decided not to leave treaty making to the Senate alone; giving the President the power to negotiate and later to make the treaty created a counterweight to the Senate and made the negotiating process less inefficient.

Constitutionalism demands limitation and diffused power, but it does not require a particular form or locus of diffusion. The loci of allocated power, however, are relevant to democracy. If, as I have suggested, the United States having become a democracy, democratic precepts should permeate our constitutional dispositions, is the treaty power, as we have it, appropriate for a democracy? Is that all the democracy that the needs of international treaty making can accommodate?

The framers gave the President a role in the treaty power when he was not to be democratically chosen and not authentically representative of or responsive and accountable to the people. Now the presidency is part of our dual democracy; he or she is elected virtually directly (though by a process weighted along state lines) and is accountable quadrennially. For the framers, the Senate's role in treaty making was not designed to serve some democratic purpose; as anti-Federalists noted at the time, the Senate was to be an aristocratic body, and it was doubtless chosen for its role in treaty making in part because of its nondemocratic character (see Introduction, p. 10). Much later, the representative character of the Senate improved with direct election (Amendment XVII) and quite recently with universal suffrage. But the Senate is still only one house of Congress, still the less representative, less accountable house, still the "aristocratic" "states' rights" branch.

One way of rendering treaty making more democratic without constitutional amendment might be to have agreements made by the President if authorized or approved by both houses of Congress, a procedure that has been called the congressional-executive agreement. It now is accepted that the congressional-executive agreement is a constitutionally acceptable alternative to the treaty method for United States adherence to any international agreement—an example of constitutional construction that developed for other reasons but could serve also the cause of greater democracy. The House has sought some such procedure for two hundred years, and the congressional-executive agreement has in fact been used regularly for some kinds of agreements —e.g., trade agreements*—but not from any concession to democratic principle and without any principle to guide choice between this method and the treaty method.

There is much—in addition to the more democratic character of that procedure for making agreements—to commend the congressional-executive agreement. Especially since treaties are automatically law or require Congress to enact implementing legislation,† treaty makers are lawmakers, and the congressional-executive agreement avoids lawmaking by less than a full, democratic legislature. Implementation, if necessary, could be accomplished at the time Congress (both houses) consented to the agreement.

Presidents might have reason to resist the congressional-executive agreement if it became the sole method of making international agreements. That method might make the process even less efficient, would double the obstacles to United States adherence (requiring consent of two houses instead of one), and increase the number of committees, members of Congress, and members of staff whose advice the executive would have to seek in order later to obtain congressional consent.‡

---

*Beginning early in our history, Congress decided that some agreements do not require Senate consent and authorized the Postmaster General to conclude international postal agreements.

†See p. 63. The congressional-executive agreement effectively gives both houses equal authority to advise and consent, therefore to veto or modify the agreement. In the case of a treaty that the President has made with Senate consent, it is established that both houses are constitutionally obligated to enact any necessary implementing legislation or appropriate any necessary funds.

‡For that reason, foreign countries — our potential treaty partners — might also not favor such a modification; they would generally prefer freer use of sole executive agreements.

On the other hand, Presidents sometimes are pleased to have a choice between the two procedures, if only in order to appease the House of Representatives and because the congressional-executive agreement does not require the concurrence of two-thirds of the Senators present. For its part, the Senate would doubtless resist a change that would eliminate its privileged status, and Senate consent would be necessary for a constitutional amendment to that end, since the Senate is part of the ordinary amending process. Without constitutional amendment, Senate consent would be necessary for establishing the congressional-executive agreement by law, and Senate consent to that procedure is in effect necessary every time the President seeks approval of an international agreement by joint resolution; the Senate can refuse to consider a joint resolution to approve an agreement and insist on the treaty procedure. But considerations of democracy (and of comity between the two Houses) might be urged upon the Senate. The Senate has accepted the joint resolution procedure for some subjects, notably trade, and it may be time for the two houses to seek—at least—to develop a general principle for identifying international agreements that might be sent to both houses for approval rather than to the Senate alone.

The treaty power as we have it is not as democratic as it might be, and without constitutional amendment it could be replaced, in whole or in part, by the congressional-executive agreement, giving the more representative House of Representatives a role equal to that of the Senate. That change would make the process more cumbersome. Do the claims of democracy demand that greater inefficiency? *

Issues as to the scope and uses of the treaty power—issues not between the President and Senate but between the treaty makers and

---

*A different issue between the President and Senate erupted when President Carter acted to terminate the defense treaty with the Republic of China [Taiwan] and to establish full relations with the People's Republic of China [Beijing]. Senators claimed that the President needed the consent of the Senate [or of Congress], and some Senators took the issue to court, but the Supreme Court did not resolve it. See *Goldwater v. Carter*, 444 U.S. 996 (1979). The Restatement has concluded that the President may terminate a treaty on his own authority, both when the treaty permits termination and when termination by the United States would violate its obligations under international law. See *Restatement (Third) Foreign Relations Law of the United States* § 339.Termination by the President alone might be suspect under the aspect of both constitutionalism and of democracy, but under the prevailing view termination is seen as an action in of the conduct of foreign relations, which has been and remains presidential even in a constitutional democracy.

It is argued with increasing frequency that a treaty settling or otherwise affecting private claims takes individual property for a public use and requires just compensation under the Fifth Amendment. (See, e.g., *Dames & Moore v. Regan*, note 5). If those arguments prevail, it may reflect enhanced concern for individual property rights and reduced concern for the public fisc and the taxpayer, in foreign affairs as elsewhere.

Congress or the states—do not significantly implicate considerations of democracy. They have virtually disappeared. It is no longer claimed that a treaty will be given effect if it violates constitutional rights, but it is not seriously argued that either principles of federalism or of separation of powers imply or warrant any limitation on the subject matter of treaties. The power to make treaties was delegated to the federal government, and neither the principle of enumerated powers nor the Tenth Amendment, which encapsulates it, nor any "invisible radiation" from that amendment warrants limiting the treaty power. No one now claims that the power to make treaties is limited by the legislative powers of Congress, though it is commonly accepted that some matters cannot be achieved by self-executing treaty but require implementation by Congress (see p. 63.) The notion that some subjects, such as a state's violation of the human rights of its inhabitants, are inherently not of international concern and therefore not within the treaty power died long ago.[8]

Treaties as Law

■ Constitutionalism and democracy are relevant to other treaty issues, involving not the President and Senate and checks and balances but the place of treaties in our constitutional jurisprudence.

The status of treaties in the constitutional system of the United States is shaped by their international character. Treaties are a principal source of international law, and the most important principle of international law is *pacta sunt servanda,* that treaties are binding and must be observed. There is, then, a binding obligation on the parties to a treaty to carry out their undertakings, but how a state does so is ordinarily not a concern of international law; the status of treaties in the domestic law of any country is a constitutional, not an international, question. All states have incorporated international law into their legal system to some extent in some ways, but states differ both as to extent and as to ways. States differ also as to what — if anything — is necessary to make a treaty part of national law and what are the jurisprudential consequences.

The United States is a hybrid of different ways and conceptions. The Constitution, Article VI, declares that treaties are law and are supreme to state law. Article VI has been interpreted as declaring also that treaties are equal to statutes in the constitutional hierarchy and therefore mandating that in case of conflict between a statute and a treaty the one which is later in time prevails.

That principle applies to only some treaties. Thanks to John Marshall, we distinguish for this purpose between self-executing treaties and non–self-executing treaties (Foster v. Neilsen, 27 U.S. (2 Pet.) 253, 314 (1829).* A treaty that is self-executing is to be applied by the executive and the courts automatically, immediately upon its entry into force for the United States. Treaties that are non–self-executing ordinarily require some implementing act, usually by Congress. As a result, as to every treaty, the executive has to decide whether it is necessary to obtain implementing legislation. Courts have to decide, when a case before them demands it, whether to give a treaty or a treaty provision effect as law or to await implementation.

Increasingly, the mood in the Senate—and in the courts—is to render, or interpret, treaties as non–self-executing and requiring implementation by Congress. This may please the House of Representatives by giving it some voice in the treaty process, and even Senators sometimes wish to have another look at a treaty in the Senate's other capacity, as a house of Congress enacting legislation. So long as we adhere to the current procedure for making treaties, however, this trend to render treaties not self-executing, I believe, is misguided. The international obligation of the United States under a treaty is immediate, whether a treaty is self-executing or not. Declaring a treaty to be non–self-executing and requiring implementing legislation delays and creates obstacles to our carrying out our international obligations and encourages members of Congress to delay or frustrate legislation to give effect to the treaty, especially Senators who did not favor the treaty and, even more, members of the House of Representatives who had not previously considered it. Little is gained, not even a second thought, since the United States has an obligation to enact necessary legislation promptly so as to enable it to carry out its obligations under the treaty.†

So long as we have self-executing treaties, we must face the possibil-

---

*It is commonly accepted that some treaties cannot be self-executing but require implementation by statute, e.g., to enact criminal law, to appropriate funds, to declare war. See *Restatement (Third) Foreign Relations, Law of the United States* § 111, Comment *i* and Reporters' Note 6.

†The argument that we should not have self-executing treaties since some other states do not misses the point. We render treaties self-executing not for the convenience of other states but to facilitate our living up to our obligations. Rendering a treaty non–self-executing in no way reduces or significantly postpones our legal obligations. See *Restatement* § 111, Reporters' Note 5.

ity of inconsistency between treaty and statute. Our jurisprudence giving treaty and statute equal status so that the later in time will prevail was developed a hundred years ago by constitutional construction based, I believe, on misconstruction of Article VI. By that article, the framers clearly intended treaties to be binding on the states and on state courts and supreme over state law, hence the appellation of Article VI as "the supremacy clause." There is no evidence that, in that article, the framers also addressed the equality of treaties and United States statutes. On the other hand, there is evidence elsewhere that, in general, the framers assumed that the United States—all the branches—would respect the Law of Nations, including treaty obligations. Certainly, there is an argument for the supremacy of international law and treaties in our jurisprudence, subject to the Constitution.

The equality of statutes and treaties, then, is not, in my view, what the framers intended and seems not to satisfy either democratic principle or international need. Democracy does not require the supremacy of laws over treaties, or even their equality, if the treaty power is itself democratic. If the Supreme Court could be persuaded to reconsider one hundred years of jurisprudence we ought to look hard at European constitutions, some of which provide for the supremacy of international law and of treaties.

Conclusion

■ Under the Constitution, treaties are made by a process unique to the United States, a special case of a larger, unique constitutional arrangement for the conduct of foreign relations, itself part of a unique congressional-presidential system. The treaty power was not designed pursuant to an ideal principle or even a working model, but is yet another of the framers' second choices. It has not worked as intended, constitutional experience having denied the Senate a full, continuing participation and relegated it to a second stage, of scrutiny and of modification or veto.

In two hundred years of history under the treaty power there have been few issues of constitutional dimension. The ABM and INF controversies of 1987–1988 masqueraded as issues of constitutional construction but were essentially, I think, reflections of political differences between independent constitutional bodies in the exercise of a shared role, which neither is pleased to share.

Neither the President nor the Senate is happy with the treaty power. The President resents Senate disposition to reject or shelve or "butcher" what he has negotiated "in the national interest." The Senate resents its being excluded from the negotiating process, being presented with a fait accompli, and being told it must take it "in the national interest." The House of Representatives is the least happy, sitting by feeling like a second-class chamber. And our partners in treaties, foreign governments, have long found the United States procedure incomprehensible and vexing, when agreements apparently concluded are frequently rejected or reopened for renegotiation.

The unhappiness of both President and Senate is particularly acute when addressing important treaties as to which both are sensitive and ambivalent. Senate unhappiness is aggravated by recognition that its role in treaty making generally terminates with consent, whereas the President and later Presidents continue to live with the treaty, interpreting and applying it. Senate unhappiness is exacerbated by fear that —as in the case of the ABM Treaty—the President, or his successor, may be tempted to weaken a treaty to which the Senate remains better disposed. Senate resentment and resistance are strong when it senses a threat to its constitutional treaty role, and they will be stronger still when it believes that the executive was not—is not—wholly forthcoming and had been—is—less than candid.

Sole executive agreements—inevitable and having their place—are not the answer to the tensions of the treaty power. The line between treaties and executive agreements that the framers would have drawn is unknown and is not a line that can be effectively determined today. Sole executive agreements, moreover, raise storm signals for constitutionalism, since such agreements entail no checks. They are also insufficiently democratic. The presidency is today a more democratic institution than the one the framers contemplated, but sole executive agreements are not authentically democratic even today; they are often secret or unknown and do not engage executive responsibility, responsiveness or accountability to the people; even the quadrennial presidential plebiscite has little relevance for them. Principles of constitutionalism and democracy suggest a limited role for sole executive agreements, especially—but not only—if an agreement entails lawmaking and affects individual rights.

The frictions of treaty making are inherent in the shared function. Recall Justice Brandeis's famous justification. "The doctrine of the separation of powers was adopted by the Convention of 1787, not to promote efficiency but to preclude the exercise of arbitrary power. The purpose was, not to avoid friction, but, by means of the inevitable friction incident to the distribution of the governmental powers among three departments, to save the people from autocracy."[9]

I know no reason to assume that Justice Brandeis would except the treaty power from that judgment. The framers did not want autocracy by treaty any more than by other executive activity. History, I think, has not proved them wrong, and transformations in the presidency, in the Senate, in the United States, in the international system, do not suggest that we should unshackle the President to make treaties without Senate consent, as by narrow construction of what is a treaty and large construction of the unwritten power to make sole executive agreements.

The treaty process needs to be thought about, but no one seems seriously to demand or contemplate change. This may come from a sense that "if it ain't broke . . ." Or perhaps treaties do not appear important enough to warrant the trouble to try to change the process of making them; perhaps unhappiness with the process is not great enough to overcome inertia; perhaps the claims of democracy are not heard; perhaps the claims of efficiency, the needs of the international system and of diplomacy, prevent our moving to a more democratic system; perhaps no better procedure seems available.

Dissatisfaction with the treaty power apart, perhaps constitutional democracy now requires that restraints on the President from considerations of constitutionalism should be lodged not in the Senate but in the House—the more representative body—or in both houses. Without formal amendment, I have suggested, we can democratize the process by increased and orderly resort to the congressional-executive agreement as an alternative to the treaty procedure. But that "solution" would please only the House and increase the unhappiness of the others concerned. That change if applied to all agreements might entail too great a sacrifice of the needs of the United States in the international system. Does democracy—our dual democracy—demand it? Or is what we have, the President combined with the Senate as they are now elected, democratic enough?

There are advantages to the congressional-executive agreement, but perhaps it is too cumbersome for general use. Perhaps we need a streamlined intermediate version. Tentatively, I venture, Congress could create a new, small, informal subconstitutional body representing both houses to deliberate together with the executive. That body would offer advice on international agreements early; consider what agreements the President could make alone in principle and whether he could make a particular agreement on his own authority; develop guidelines for deciding between the treaty method and the congressional-executive agreement and apply them in particular cases; and decide whether an agreement should be self-executing or require legislative implementation.

Together, the House and the Senate, as the legislature, might also regulate and scrutinize sole executive agreements. The executive now reports the executive agreements it has made; does anyone look at them? Better scrutiny of what the executive has done might lead to greater caution by the executive in deciding not to seek the approval of the Senate or of Congress. In turn, it might well lead also to more orderly delegation to the President by Congress of authority to conclude agreements, thereby effectively converting all agreements into congressional-executive agreements as a matter of constitutional authority but without the cumbersomeness of that process.

Subject to such tinkering or tuning, in the complex governmental system we have, we may be "stuck with" the treaty-making procedure we have. As the framers recognized, Congress cannot negotiate. As history has demonstrated, we cannot return to formal advice by the Senate as a whole. Although it developed from other considerations, the treaty-making process the framers gave us, even as it has been modified by experience, does not in principle clearly offend constitutionalism or democracy. But we will continue to have crises unless both President and Senate take care to make the present procedure, or a congressional-executive alternative, work. We need to move toward greater cooperation and less adversariness between the branches, but that is easy to recommend and difficult to achieve in a system of independent branches. The advice function ought to be reintroduced, not formally but regularly, and should include some advice on important sole executive agreements. Later Presidents must not attempt to shave treaty obligations by reinterpretation (or misinterpretation). The ABM controversy should not tempt the Senate to load its consent with express understandings, to clutter treaties with conditions, to jam the treaty process. In relations between them concerning treaties, the President must be candid, the Senate must be restrained.

This is not a cheerful or ringing conclusion, but it is — I think — the message of the still, small voice of the Constitution we have inherited and are devoted to, in our kind of constitutional democracy in a world of states.

3

THE COURTS IN FOREIGN AFFAIRS

■

For the framers, the courts constituted the third branch of government, "the least dangerous" branch, Hamilton said, since it "has no influence over either the sword or the purse."[1] Over two-hundred years, however, still without sword or purse, the courts have won the struggle for judicial supremacy, and the courts as supreme, infallible guardians of the Constitution[2] are the hallmark of United States constitutionalism and the envy of many political societies around the world.

It may seem supererogatory, then, to ask about the adequacy of the judiciary in our governance for the third century of the Constitution. But whatever its appeal in other quarters of the world, the propriety of the judicial role and the legitimacy of judicial supremacy are recurrently challenged in the United States, again recently and in high places and in some academic halls. Where I am looking, moreover—governance of our foreign affairs—the judicial role is different and smaller; exceptionally, the courts have removed themselves to a backseat and have not played a major part in that governance.

For present purposes, I take as given the familiar constitutional role of the courts generally in the federal system: as Article III courts deciding cases arising under the Constitution, laws and treaties, and other designated cases or controversies, and the courts as monitors and calibrators of the constitutional system, sometimes summarized as "judicial review." My purpose is to explore respects in which the general role of the courts has been different in foreign affairs; to ask whether there is good reason for such differences; to ask, too, whether the framers' concern for constitutionalism and our emerged democracy are adequately reflected in the judicial role today. In a word, what is the proper role for the courts as regards foreign affairs in our constitutional republic now that it has become a democracy?

Many a case coming to court because it arises under the Constitution, laws, and treaties of the United States and many another case or controversy within the judicial power impinge on the foreign affairs of the United States. In the course of their decisions, courts scrutinize the constitutional validity of acts of Congress or of actions of the executive branch that affect United States foreign relations, interpret such acts of Congress or treaties of the United States, and determine and apply international law (also known as the law of nations); at times, the courts even make some law related to foreign affairs on their own authority, e.g., the Act of State doctrine.*

Judicial Deference

■ The words *foreign affairs* do not appear in the Constitution, and there is nothing in the Constitution or in the intent of the framers to suggest that foreign affairs are a discrete constitutional category for the courts any more than for the other branches of government.

Yet where foreign affairs are concerned, the courts have learned to carry out their normal functions with due—I think sometimes undue —deference to the political branches. Deference is not only avowed but is made a principle of decision. The reasons for deference are not often articulated and are rarely examined, but high among them appears to be some sense that the governmental act in question may implicate the national interest in relation to other nations, if not na-

---

*The courts have established that they will not sit in judgment on acts of government of a foreign state done within its own territory.

tional security, and that in foreign affairs the United States must "speak with a single voice" and that voice must be that of the experts, usually the executive branch. Some such uncertain blend of patriotism with judicial humility no doubt underlies rules of deference to executive interpretations of treaties (and the act of state doctrine; see p. 70). It is to be found also, I think, in sometimes extravagant judicial interpretations of statutes in order to support a conclusion that a questionable executive act was done by authority of Congress.[3] Even in judging political acts in the light of constitutional norms, both legislative and executive power in foreign affairs are construed largely. Where "balancing" an individual right against the public interest is deemed to be the constitutional order, courts treat foreign affairs differently: private rights are depreciated, while competing public needs are accorded compelling weight. For example, the Court decided that freedom of travel abroad is protected less than freedom of domestic travel and gave greater weight to the national interest in limiting foreign travel.[4] In such balancing, the Court provided no standard for measuring either individual right or public interest, and its method has seemed essentially impressionistic, some might say lawless; surely it gives no guidance to lower courts and only encourages them to improvise, too. Immigration laws and their executive implementations, and particularly those governing exclusion and deportation, remain virtually exempt from meaningful judicial review under the Constitution.[5]

In a different context, although courts apply international law as the law of the land, although the Constitution declares it to be the President's duty to take care that the law be faithfully executed, courts have given effect to executive actions that they accepted as being in violation of international law, merely because the Attorney General had approved those actions.* We are not told why or on what theory; we are not told whether that is a general principle or is so only in the case of *some* international norms and *some* executive actions.

I do not, I think, underestimate the importance of foreign affairs and the expertise, or bona fides, of the executive branch; nor do I overestimate the competence of the courts. But I do not share the view

---

*In 1986, lower courts found that the detention of thousands of undocumented aliens for years violated international law, but they accepted the right of the executive to violate international law and refused to enjoin it (*Garcia-Mir v. Meese*, 788 F.2d 1446 (11th Cir.), *cert. denied*, 479 U.S. 886 [1986]). That decision is difficult to understand. There was no claim that the President had special constitutional authority to incarcerate people. Why should the Court refuse to enforce international law?

that foreign affairs are always "special" for constitutional purposes. In my view the easy blanketing of "national security or foreign policy" — as in some executive regulations — is pernicious. Not every issue touching on foreign affairs is a question of "war or peace"; not every action plausibly related to the vague contours of national security is compelling or weighty enough to warrant infringement of important individual rights. Nor is there always a compelling need for judicial deference to the executive in the interpretation of statutes. Courts are no more competent, but no less competent, to construe an act of Congress relating to foreign affairs than they are, say, laws relating to the national economy or the national environment. And Congress, which — inevitably — leaves the interpretation of statutes to the executive, also — inevitably — leaves review of executive interpretation to the courts, in foreign affairs as elsewhere.

Legislation on foreign affairs is the responsibility of Congress, and the conduct of foreign relations is entrusted to the executive. Both branches have broad powers, and there is rarely any ground for challenging the authority exercised by either branch as unconstitutional. Ordinarily, the appropriate judicial reply to a challenge to an act of Congress or to an executive action is that the political branch acted within its constitutional authority. But there is no warrant for the courts to be mesmerized by incantations of "national interest" or "national security." There is reason for due deference to the executive, but not for undue deference — for due judicial humility, but not undue humility.

Here I focus principally on "judicial review," the responsibility of the courts to scrutinize governmental action to assure their conformity to the Constitution. The Constitution, we know, does not explicitly provide for judicial review* and therefore, of course, is not explicit as to the application of judicial review in foreign affairs. Nor has constitutional jurisprudence developed a principle that foreign affairs are not subject or are less subject or even differently subject to judicial review. But judicial review has in fact been applied in foreign affairs with some difference.

To begin, in matters of foreign affairs the courts have a different perspective on constitutional text. The Supreme Court, we shall see (see p. 74), has declared that, as regards foreign affairs, the constitu-

---

*There were even great men, notably Judge Learned Hand, (see L. Hand, *The Bill of Rights* [1958]), who questioned whether the framers intended it, but it is now firmly established as essential to our constitutional system.

tional text is incomplete and it is necessary to refer elsewhere to complete the definition of our constitutional system. The courts, I have suggested, give extraordinary weight to national interest in foreign affairs at the expense of individual rights. And they have developed a special doctrine of judicial abstention from review—the political question doctrine—and applied it to reduce judicial review, particularly in foreign affairs.

Judicial Review

■ We have recently endured once again sharp division as to the proper role of the courts in our constitutional governance. We hear once again attempts to put into question the legitimacy of the judicial role as the final arbiter of the Constitution and as supreme monitor of the constitutionality of governmental action. No one has seriously—at least not openly—urged the abolition of what has become the glory of the American constitutional system and the basis for its admiration (indeed, envy) around the world. But some have decried judicial review as antidemocratic and have urged modes of construction and prudential doctrines that would sharply circumscribe it. I do not propose to revisit the controversy about judicial review that has pitted "interpretivists" against "noninterpretivists"—those who see the courts' task as limited to applying and interpreting the written text and original intent, as against those who see the courts in a larger function, applying a larger conception of the Constitution, permitting—indeed, requiring—the Court to develop and apply a "living Constitution." For our purposes, that controversy is largely beside the point. For the deep issues of foreign affairs—notably those of the "twilight zone" discussed above—there is little or no text to construe and what is there is hopelessly opaque and nondeterminative. Looking at that text or elsewhere for the intent of the framers—however one defines and identifies them—is no more helpful, for their intent is unknown or hopelessly ambiguous.

In foreign affairs, moreover, the Supreme Court has authoritatively declared the text to be incomplete and inadequate. I remind you of the Supreme Court's nearly unanimous essay in *U.S. v. Curtiss-Wright Export Corp:*

It results that the investment of the federal government with the powers of external sovereignty did not depend upon the affirmative grants of the Constitution. The powers to declare and wage war, to conclude peace, to make treaties, to maintain diplomatic relations with other sovereignties, if they had never been mentioned in the Constitution, would have vested in the federal government as necessary concomitants of nationality. . . . As a member of the family of nations, the right and power of the United States in that field are equal to the right and power of the other members of the international family. Otherwise, the United States is not completely sovereign. The power to acquire territory by discovery and occupation . . . the power to expel undesirable aliens . . ., the power to make such international agreements as do not constitute treaties in the constitutional sense . . . none of which is expressly affirmed by the Constitution, nevertheless exist as inherently inseparable from the conception of nationality. This the court recognized, and . . . found the warrant for its conclusions not in the provisions of the Constitution, but in the law of nations (299 U.S. 304, 318 [1936]).

The Court there declared the text of the Constitution insufficient for purposes of defining the powers of the federal government; it thereby effectively declared it insufficient also for determining the respective authority of the political branches of the federal government where it is not explicitly provided. The Constitution allocates power to the federal government by allocating it to one branch of the federal government or another. If, under *Curtiss-Wright,* the federal government has powers not enumerated in the Constitution, the Constitution provides no guidance as to how such powers are distributed between Congress and the President. As a result, we refer to "the foreign affairs powers" of Congress, unenumerated and undefined; we refer to "the foreign affairs powers" of the President, also unenumerated and undefined.

Thanks, then, to the flimsiness of constitutional text and to Justice Sutherland in *Curtiss-Wright,* we are all fated to be largely "noninterpretivists" in foreign affairs. (One might say that the unenumerated powers of the federal government have a "legislative" component belonging to Congress and an "executive" component belonging to the President, but that is hardly a formula that affords certainty and avoids dispute between Congress and the President. And in foreign affairs we do not hear many calls to return to the intent of the framers. See p. 123 above.) Those — including some judges — who see the only justification for judicial review to be a written text committed to the courts' care might conclude that since there is little text, there is little need or place for judicial review in foreign affairs. That conclusion, I submit, is wholly without warrant, for it overlooks the basis of the judicial role in our constitutional governance.

In the recurrent debates about the legitimacy, mode, and scope of judicial review, I have missed—on both sides—significant attention to the theoretical foundations and justifications of judicial review as a reflection of the political theory of the Constitution. Put bluntly, there has been much discussion of the legitimacy of judicial review; I have missed discussion of the contemporary legitimacy of the Constitution that the courts apply. Both sides seem to accept judicial review as established by positive law, as itself prescribed by text, original intent, and history. Both sides seem to seek to determine the modes and the limits of judicial review by reference to the text (Articles III and VI), to the framers' intent, and to history. The Constitution, we know, declares its own supremacy, and the Supreme Court, we know, applies the Constitution as supreme law. But why is the Constitution supreme today? Why are text and original intent or, for that matter, history and noninterpretivist values determinative of what is supreme law today?

It may be that the Constitution is supreme merely because it has been accepted as such by our political culture. We have inherited the Constitution as we have inherited other federal law. And we also inherit and accept its supremacy and its immutability unless amended by the procedures it sets forth. Similarly, then, we accept judicial review because we inherited it as part of our constitutional system and have not been moved to reject it. Or perhaps we accept it because we like it, because we think it "works."

That, I believe, is not what the Constitution implies or what the framers intended. For the framers, as I suggested (see p. 4) the supremacy of the Constitution was inherent in its character, and it had authentic justification in their political theory. The Constitution was their social contract, and its supremacy was implicit in that contract. For them, it was decided early,[6] judicial review was part of the contract and the means for assuring that the political branches acted in conformity with the contract.

Today we are entitled to ask whether and why the social contract of our ancestors is binding on us. I have suggested elsewhere that if the Constitution is a social compact and the legitimacy of government depends on that compact, its legitimacy today depends on the Constitution being *our* compact, not only the compact of our ancestors.* For the framers, that compact expressed a commitment to constitutionalism—to limited government, to checks and balances, to retained rights. If the same compact is our compact, we too are committed to that constitutionalism—to limited government, to checks and balances, to retained rights. For the framers, judicial review was an instrument of constitutionalism; judicial review is an instrument of constitutionalism for us, too.

We hear much about the undemocratic—indeed, antidemocratic—character of judicial review. To the framers, the fact that the courts were not democratic was wholly irrelevant. They were republicans, I have said, not democrats (see p. 8); surely, they put republicanism above democracy and subjected both to individual rights. For them, courts were the instruments of constitutionalism. Indeed, constitutionalism for the framers was, inter alia, a safeguard against the excesses of democracy,† and the courts early became one of the instruments of their antidemocracy. We, two hundred years later, perhaps by redefining democracy, have abandoned the framers' resistance to democracy in principle and indeed have embraced and exalted democracy, but our commitment, too, is to democracy subject to constitutionalism, subject to checks and balances and individual rights. For us too, then, the Court is the guarantor of constitutionalism, even when constitutionalism limits democracy. It is not the courts but the Constitution that, narrowly conceived, is antidemocratic.‡ The courts are the ultimate guardians of the Constitution, even to the extent that it is antidemocratic.

In fact, I think, seeing the Constitution and judicial review as antidemocratic is specious. It is indeed appropriate for us to recognize that judicial review, when it results in invalidating a legislative act, frustrates the will and overrides the judgment of the legislature, the principal contemporary representatives of our democracy. But the framers did not see such judicial review as invalidating the will of the people. They

---

*Thomas Paine said: "The vanity and presumption of governing beyond the grave, is the most ridiculous and insolent of all tyrannies." *The Rights of Man,* H. Collins, ed. (Pelican Classic Edition), pp. 63–64.

†See *The Federalist Papers,* no. 10 (J. Madison).

‡Its antidemocratic character is epitomized in the first words of our Bill of Rights: "Congress shall make no law . . . ," a provision that would have been unheard of in England and other countries committed to parliamentary supremacy. When the Bill of Rights was drafted, Congress was not a democratic institution by our lights. Now Congress is more authentically democratic, but we are determined nonetheless that "Congress shall make no law . . ."

saw the Constitution, too—or the Constitution in particular—as representing the will of the people. One might say they saw the Constitution as representing the people as "constitutors," whereas the legislature represents the people in a lesser capacity, the people as legislators. Appeal to the Constitution, then, is not antidemocratic; it is an appeal to the people as constitutors, sometimes even against the people as legislators. The courts represent the people in their authentic sovereign capacity, the people as constitutors.

By our lights, the people in the framers' generation were not adequately represented in either capacity. Few of them voted or were permitted to vote for delegates to the bodies that produced and ratified the Constitution; few of them voted or were permitted to vote for even one house of Congress, the House of Representatives, and none of them voted or were permitted to vote for Senators or for the President. Today all of us can vote. All the people accept the Constitution and are represented by it; today all the people are represented in the legislature and by the President. Far better than in the framers' generation, then, the courts today can be seen as representatives of democracy when they represent all the people in monitoring their Constitution. The legislature (and the executive) might claim that they too are responsible to the Constitution and to the people as constitutors; they too take the oath to support the Constitution, and they too can decide what the Constitution means. That, indeed, is their responsibility in the first instance. But the people have reposed their confidence in the independence, impartiality, and wisdom of the judiciary and in its insulation from the political process. In the second instance, ultimately, it is the courts who represent the Constitution and the people as constitutors.

In foreign affairs, moreover, judicial review rarely invalidates the will of the legislature. There have been few invalidations of any act of Congress of any kind in half a century; there has been none in foreign affairs in all of our history. The courts, then, do not in fact frustrate the will of the people as represented by Congress. In foreign affairs, judicial review addresses not legislative but executive acts. Even accepting the constitutional fiction that every one of the millions of anonymous, "faceless" executive officials is "the President" for constitutional purposes, it is not obvious that invalidating an executive action is an antidemocratic act. Surely it is not antidemocratic to invalidate an executive act on the ground that it usurps the power of Congress or flouts an act of Congress. Nor is it obvious that the executive branch is generally a more democratic instrumentality than the judiciary. At our beginnings as a nation, surely, both the executive and the judiciary were "elected" indirectly. The President was no more representative, no more responsible, no more accountable to the people than were the courts. Today, none of the members of the executive branch, other than the President, is elected by the people except in the most indirect fictional sense. And if we accept the President's quadrennial election as "democratic," contemporary events may warrant some doubt as to the effectiveness of that election as Presidential accountability in foreign affairs and therefore as guarantees of a democratic foreign policy. On the other hand, it must be granted, the selection of judges remains indirect and life terms make judges less accountable. But that does not necessarily render the courts less "democratic." The constitutional system that the people today desire prescribes life tenure for judges and affords them other guarantees of independence and political insulation, in order to assure that they can carry out their representative function of protecting our constitutionalism.

The arguments for less, rather than more, judicial review are no more persuasive where foreign affairs are involved. Here, since we are all noninterpretivists, the special expertise of courts in reading text, one must admits, is not relevant; but judges are perhaps better qualified than the political branches to read what is relevant, including constitutional history and constitutional experience. In any event, judges are better ultimate monitors of constitutionalism and of the constitutional system and better ultimate guardians of individual rights, in foreign affairs as elsewhere.

It is our two-hundred-year (and more) commitment to constitutionalism that demands judicial review. Our constitutionalism is framed in holy text and in the institutions it established, and we have to look at the text when there is text. But that constitutionalism is more than the particulars that emerged from eighteenth-century political sociology and from compromises in Philadelphia. Where the text does not specify and is not complete (as *Curtiss-Wright* concludes), "where fairly possible" (as Justice Brandeis once put it in a related context),[7] the principles of constitutionalism ought to govern, and the courts have been chosen to help make them prevail.

Judicial review is necessary in foreign affairs, at least as much as elsewhere, to assure that we are a *constitutional* democracy. Courts ought to exercise that task in foreign affairs, at least as effectively as elsewhere. I am therefore troubled by the increasing tendency of courts not to hear foreign affairs issues, even constitutional issues, or otherwise to avoid constitutional scrutiny, a tendency that has infected judicial practice particularly in foreign affairs.

Courts and Constitutionalism: Political Questions

■ Consider the courts' jurisprudence of judicial review.

The Constitution did not explicitly declare the finality and supremacy of the Supreme Court. John Marshall seized an occasion to assert the power to declare an act of Congress unconstitutional in a suit by a private person claiming a private right, and Marshall claimed that he had no choice but to consider the validity of the act of Congress in order to decide the case before the Court. Perhaps for that reason judicial review grew slowly, hesitantly, and not without uncertainty as to the finality and supremacy of the Court's decision. Perhaps for that reason judicial review was sometimes resisted by the other branches; perhaps for that reason the courts themselves sometimes have been hesitant to exercise judicial review, invoking a mode of self-restraint, developing doctrines for not deciding constitutional issues, some of which they read into constitutional text, others admittedly reflecting their own sense of prudence.

In time, judicial review became an established feature of the constitutional system. The Court was accepted as the monitor of our constitutionalism, of federalism, of separation of powers, and of individual rights. The Court became the calibrater and adjuster of the Constitution's parts, updating its eighteenth-century dispositions. But the modes and procedures of judicial review remained those Marshall assumed and others developed.

I have been confused by the Supreme Court's jurisprudence of not hearing constitutional issues, beginning with the requirement of "case or controversy." It is interesting to recall that one of the underpinnings of the jurisprudence on case or controversy involved foreign affairs— the refusal by the Justices to provide advisory opinions to President Washington in matters relating to foreign affairs.[8] The Justices thought such a practice would be inappropriate, inconsistent with the separation of powers and checks and balances; their view was that judicial power should be limited to the judicial function. Perhaps, indeed, the framers did not contemplate that the courts should give advice to the President or perform other nonjudicial roles.[9] But I have not been satisfied that the reference in the Constitution to "cases" and to "controversies" was intended to impose the strict and sharp limitation on federal judicial jurisdiction that it has become or that it needs to be construed as restrictively as it has been.

I will not add to the confusion of the rest of the jurisprudence for not hearing cases—the requirements of standing, ripeness, nonmootness, concreteness—all of which have had recent foreign affairs applications.[10] "Standing" in particular, however, continues to live in uncertainty, and in foreign affairs we have had a new class of plaintiffs claiming the right to litigate in a stream of cases:[11] (Senator) *Goldwater v. Carter;* (Representative) *Edwards v. Carter;* (Senator) *Dole v. Carter;* (Representative) *Crockett v. Reagan;* (Representative) *Lowry v. Reagan;* (Representative) *Conyers v. Reagan;* (Senator) *Cranston v. Reagan,* et al.* The standing of members of Congress, in general or in a particular context, has not been seriously considered; that they ought to be accorded standing in many of the cases in which they have asserted it is not obvious, but the Supreme Court has not told us whether and when and why they should or should not have standing.

As our adjudicatory system based on case or controversy has developed, important constitutional issues ordinarily are not brought to court by the institutions principally affected. Issues of federalism—say, a claim that Congress had exercised power not delegated to it and had invaded the reserved powers of the states—are at bottom issues between the United States and the states, as Kentucky and Virginia declared when they adopted their nullification resolutions. But under our jurisprudence, such a claim can be brought before the courts by a private person but *not* by a state,[12] nor by all the states together, and not by the people (the party to the constitutional social compact). Similarly, we do not have suits between Congress and the President to litigate issues of separation of powers or checks and balances.

I confess to some difficulties with a jurisprudence that in principle does not accept suits by *The Congress v. The President,* but accepts one by *Several Members of Congress v. The President* for precisely the same

---

* Each of these plaintiff members of Congress represented himself as well as many other members, in one case 110 of them.

issue between the branches. But I do not see insuperable obstacles or compelling reasons why an issue between Congress and the President should not be decided by the courts in a case between them, as the same issue would be decided if it were involved in a private suit.[13] Perhaps instead of random suits by self-appointed members of Congress, speciously on their own behalf, it would be preferable for Congress to develop a procedure for authorizing suits by some members on behalf of Congress (and also arrange to have suits against Congress properly defended).

For the present, we have a proliferation of suits by members of Congress.* The growth of congressional standing reflects perhaps the intractability of the issues between Congress and President discussed earlier (chapter 1). Members of Congress turn to the courts as a last resort, and the courts, reluctant to close off that last resort, grant standing. But after granting standing, the lower courts have been refusing relief, often on the ground that the issue raised is a "political," not a justiciable, question. I leave issues of congressional standing for another forum; I address the political question doctrine in the light of the judicial function in a constitutional democracy.

■ What is the political question doctrine?

In its authentic sense, it is a judicial policy declaring that certain cases, or questions in cases, that are within the constitutional and statutory jurisdiction of the federal courts and that otherwise meet all the requirements and indicia for adjudication are nonetheless nonjusticiable.

A dozen years ago, I asked: "Is there a political question doctrine?"[14] I suggested that it was all a mistake—in two senses: there was no jurisprudential basis for it, and it was undesirable. I urged that the doctrine be abandoned and that its few authentic and worthy components be assigned elsewhere, to other doctrines. I have not repented. But the intervening years have made it clear that the courts—and especially the executive branch — are enamored of the doctrine; and it is likely that it will be with us at least for some years into our third century.

---

*There have also been suits by the President challenging congressional legislation in special circumstances, (e.g., *Nixon v. Administrator of General Services*, 433 U.S. 425 [1977]; compare *Senate Select Committee on Presidential Campaign Activities v. Nixon*, 370 F. Supp. 521 [D.D.C. 1974]), but not to litigate issues of alleged usurpation by Congress of presidential authority.

The Supreme Court reconsidered the political question doctrine nearly thirty years ago in *Baker v. Carr.*[15] In that case, involving a constitutional challenge to legislative malapportionment, the Court found the political question doctrine inapplicable and ordered the case to be adjudicated. But the Court thought to bring order into a chaotic field by another of its periodic "clean-up" essays and gave us "the *Baker* formula." In doing so, the Court gave the doctrine new life, and it did not eliminate but only confounded confusion. Foreign affairs is where the doctrine flourishes and where confusion about it is rampant.

Which questions are political, not justiciable? I remind you of the *Baker* formula:

> It is apparent that several formulations which vary slightly according to the settings in which the questions arise may describe a political question, although each has one or more elements which identify it as essentially a function of the separation of powers. Prominent on the surface of any case held to involve a political question is found a textually demonstrable constitutional commitment of the issue to a coordinate political department; or a lack of judicially discoverable and manageable standards for resolving it; or the impossibility of deciding without an initial policy determination of a kind clearly for nonjudicial discretion; or the impossibility of a court's undertaking independent resolution without expressing lack of the respect due coordinate branches of government; or an unusual need for unquestioning adherence to a political decision already made; or the potentiality of embarrassment from multifarious pronouncements by various departments on one question.[16]

Government officials invoke the political question doctrine, and the *Baker* formula, routinely, ritually, in virtually every foreign affairs case brought against the President or against some executive department or official.* The lower courts often reject the doctrine, but too often apply it, citing one clause or another in the *Baker* formula. My impression is that the lower courts have found issues to be political and nonjusticiable more often during the past twenty-five years since *Baker* than in all our previous history. On appeal, the political question ground is frequently rejected and the court will say, as in a recent case, "reliance on the political question doctrine is misplaced."[17] But they

---

*The executive branch did not consider foreign affairs issues nonjusticiable when it sought an order to close an observer mission to the United Nations. Congress has had occasion to invoke the doctrine only infrequently, but it too has not been averse to doing so, as when it sought to prevent adjudication of the validity of the "legislative veto." (*United States v. Palestine Liberation Organization,* 695 F. Supp. 1456 [S.D.N.Y.] (1988); *INS v. Chadha,* 462 U.S. 919 [1983]).

do not indicate why it is misplaced. (The refusal to adjudicate is frequently affirmed on other grounds.)

The Supreme Court has steadfastly rejected or avoided the claim that an issue is political and nonjusticiable.[18] Once or twice the Supreme Court made "political question" sounds,[19] but it has not held anything to be an authentic "political question" since *Baker*, indeed, since 1938, in an idiosyncratic case, not involving foreign affairs.[20] But the Supreme Court has not revisited the *Baker* formulations. The Court has not told us what any of the clauses in *Baker* means, in what context it is to be applied, and why it renders a question nonjusticiable.

In 1979, some additional guidance — some of his colleagues thought misguidance — was offered by Justice Rehnquist in *Goldwater v. Carter*.[21] The Senate had challenged President Carter's authority to terminate the defense treaty with the Republic of China (Taiwan) without the concurrence of Congress or of the Senate. Senator Goldwater and nineteen other Senators brought President Carter to court. The lower courts held that the Senators had standing to bring the suit. The Court of Appeals decided that the issue was not a political question, that it had to decide the case, and ruled that the President had the power to terminate the treaty. The Supreme Court upheld the Senators' claim to standing without much discussion, but a majority of the Court refused to consider whether under the Constitution the President had power to terminate the treaty. Four Justices—less than a majority—said it was a political question: Justice Rehnquist wrote that the Court should not decide the case because "we are asked to settle a dispute between coequal branches of our Government, each of which has resources available to protect and assert its interests, resources not available to private litigants outside the judicial forum."[22] In effect, the four Justices apparently would hold that an issue of separation of powers is not for the courts to decide, at least when litigated between the two branches. Justice Brennan, author of *Baker v. Carr*, told his four brethren that they "profoundly misapprehend[ed]" the political question doctrine.[23]

It has never been clear to me why Justice Rehnquist, et al., thought the issue in that case nonjusticiable. Questions of alleged usurpation of power by the President (or by Congress; see p. 82) have been decided by the Court in other cases, e.g., the *Steel Seizure* case,[24] and the wisdom of deciding that case, or such issues, has not been questioned. There private interests brought suit; in *Goldwater* members of Congress brought suit. The Court might have said that they had "no standing" because members of Congress have no justiciable interest; on the question of standing it may be relevant and material that Congress has its weapons and need not bring its battles to court. But the political question doctrine has it that an *issue* is not justiciable, presumably even if raised by a private person. Perhaps the four Justices did not know and were not sure where to find the answer to the substantive question —whether the President had power to terminate a treaty. Other Justices apparently did not think that to be a sufficient reason for not deciding. Justice Brennan decided the issue. The Court of Appeals decided this issue. The Supreme Court would presumably have found the answer if the issue had been raised in a suit by a private person, as the Court did in the *Steel Seizure* case and in several recent "separation" cases that had no obvious answer.[25]

Goldwater apart, the Supreme Court has avoided considering political question cases, but in the lower courts the political question doctrine has had a busy life. A large number of cases involved challenges to the President's power to use force, the big issue in the twilight zone that continues to trouble our polity and our jurisprudence. (See chapter 1) That issue began to come to court during the Vietnam War, not long after *Baker v. Carr*. Soldiers claimed that they could not be sent to the war because the President had no constitutional authority to wage the war and Congress had not authorized it. The courts were divided: some said that the President had been given authority by Congress; some said the question was not justiciable. In my view, Congress had in fact authorized that war in the Tonkin Gulf Resolution and the war was therefore within the President's authority delegated to him by Congress. If so, the courts properly rejected the soldiers' objection. But a number of courts refused to consider the claim, denying the plaintiffs judicial consideration of their claim of a serious violation of important rights, which, I think, did not help assuage disaffection in a time of acute national malaise.[26]

The war powers have come to court in numerous other cases since the Vietnam War, several arising out of events in Central America during this decade. Representative Conyers and others challenged the authority of President Reagan to send United States armed forces into Grenada in 1983, claiming that the President had usurped congressional war power. Representative Crockett and others sought declaratory and injunctive relief against United States military involvement in

El Salvador, claiming that the President had violated congressional legislation. In *Sanchez-Espinoza*, plaintiffs, including several residents of Nicaragua, twelve members of Congress, and residents of Florida, charged that by engaging in military activities against Nicaragua the President had usurped the war powers of Congress and had also flouted laws of the United States, notably the War Powers Resolution and the Boland Amendment. The Committee of U.S. Citizens Living in Nicaragua recently sought injunctive and declaratory relief against the funding of the Contras to fight in Nicaragua. And in a "war power" issue in a different part of the world, in *Lowry v. Reagan*, one hundred and ten members of Congress claimed that the President had failed to comply with the War Powers Resolution when he deployed naval vessels in the Persian Gulf during the Iraq-Iran War.[27]

In 1985, Women of Greenham Common, England, sued in United States courts to challenge the deployment of nuclear weapons in their backyards. It is interesting that the court found that the plaintiffs had standing, apparently because it accepted that the United States Constitution applies to an act by United States authorities even in the territory of another state. That court apparently saw the Constitution as not only a compact by citizens for citizens, but as establishing a community of conscience requiring the government to respect constitutional limitations wherever it acts.[28] Then, however, the court proceeded to dismiss the claim. The court might have said that the President had authority pursuant to the North Atlantic Treaty to deploy weapons in the United Kingdom with the consent of the United Kingdom and that no constitutional right was violated by such deployment. Instead, the court said the matter was a "political question," and refused to consider the claim.[29]

Perhaps the courts did not have to consider the constitutional claims brought by members of Congress because, arguably, they had no personal, justiciable interest. Perhaps the courts should have held in all those cases that the President had authority to do what he did, authority acquired over two-hundred-years of history. (See chapter 1) Perhaps, even if the courts were to conclude that the President had no constitutional authority, they might decide not to grant some particular remedy or any remedy, since courts had traditionally exercised such discretion. But why are the questions not justiciable? I have similar difficulties with the notion that a claim that the President was flouting an act of Congress is not justiciable. The courts daily mandate the executive branch to "take care that the laws [of Congress] be faithfully executed," and I know no reason why they should not do so for laws that regulate war-making or other activities related to our foreign relations.

There have been foreign affairs cases not involving war powers that prompted resort to the political question doctrine. In 1977, Senator Dole sued to enjoin the implementation of an agreement by President Carter to return the crown of Saint Stephen to Hungary, on the ground that he had made a treaty without Senate consent. The Court of Appeals found no justiciable controversy.[30] In 1986, plaintiffs sued to enjoin the President from establishing diplomatic relations with the Vatican, on the ground, inter alia, that it would violate the First Amendment, in particular, the prohibition of the establishment of religion. The District Court dismissed on the ground that a presidential decision to establish diplomatic relation with a foreign state presents a nonjusticiable political question; the Court of Appeals for the Third Circuit affirmed.[31]

I do not understand. In fact, I do not think that the President's decision in that case violated the nonestablishment clause; I have difficulty hypothesizing a plausible situation in which a decision to establish diplomatic relations with a foreign state would violate any provision of the Constitution. I might have dismissed that case for want of a substantial federal question or even as frivolous. But why is it nonjusticiable? Another plaintiff brought a taxpayer's suit to challenge the constitutionality of a statute authorizing military assistance to Israel on the ground that it violated the same clause of the First Amendment (because, the complaint said, Israel has an establishment of religion).[32] There are many reasons for dismissing that complaint, including the fact that the argument is silly. But why isn't the issue justiciable?

Pursuant to an agreement with the Government of Haiti, the President ordered the United States Coast Guard to interdict Haitian and American vessels on the high seas suspected of bringing undocumented aliens to the United States. The Coast Guard interdicted such vessels and, after a perfunctory hearing to determine whether passengers were refugees entitled to refugee status under United States law, returned them to Haiti. In a suit on their behalf in the federal courts, the plaintiffs claimed, inter alia, that they had been deprived of their liberty without due process of law and had been effectively denied the legislative right to a determination of refugee status and a grant of asylum.

Again the U.S. Government argued that the issue was a political question. (The courts rejected the suit on other grounds.)[33] Why shouldn't the courts consider such claims? And why shouldn't courts consider a claim by a United States citizen residing in Honduras that the United States military had taken his property there for public use without just compensation? In the end, a majority of the Court of Appeals held the issue justiciable, over strong dissent.[34]

In sum, I do not understand the political question doctrine. I see no basis for a court not deciding a case when the court has jurisdiction, when a plaintiff who satisfies the requirements of case or controversy, standing, ripeness, concreteness, etc., challenges the constitutionality of an act of Congress or challenges an executive act as not within the President's authority under the Constitution or laws. Surely, there is no constitutional basis, textual or otherwise, for a doctrine that would deny judicial review to an individual who claims that one of the political branches had usurped a constitutional power or had denied him or her a constitutional right.* The political question doctrine has no basis in the Constitution. It is indeed arguable, as Professor Herbert Wechsler argued, that it is anticonstitutional.[35] Early, Justice John Marshall said: "It is most true that this court will not take jurisdiction if it should not; but it is equally true, that it must take jurisdiction if it should. . . . The one or the other would be treason to the constitution."[36] I think that to refuse to decide on the ground of the political question doctrine is in many instances in essence the same as not to take jurisdiction. By calling a claim a political question courts foster the perception that it is not a constitutional question and encourage the exercise of political power without regard to constitutional prescriptions and restraints.

If it is not treason to the Constitution, the political question doctrine may betray constitutionalism. As applied to constitutional questions, the doctrine is an abandonment by the judiciary of its role as monitor of the constitutional system. By applying the doctrine in such cases, the courts condone a breach in the wall of checks and balances

*There are one or two clauses in the Constitution that can perhaps be interpreted as denying judicial scrutiny of certain political acts. "Each House shall be the judge of the Elections, Returns and Qualifications its own Members" (Art. 1, sec. 5) may be read as meaning that each house shall be the "sole judge" and denying a judicial role. Or "the Senate shall have the sole power to try all impeachments" (Art. 1, sec. 3) may be interpreted as meaning that nothing about the trial of an impeachment may be reviewed in a court. My colleague Professor Wechsler so argued. The courts have not in fact followed him, but in any event, those clauses do not raise issues frequently and are not related to foreign affairs. *Roudebush v. Hartke*, 405 U.S. 15 (1972); *Powell v. McCormack*, 395 U.S. 486 (1969); compare *United States v. Nixon*, 418 U.S. 683 (1974).

or the violation of individual rights and encourage lawlessness. When the courts refuse to decide a claim of usurpation by the President of legislative power, they abdicate their function of preserving constitutionalism as well as our dual democracy. They abdicate that function as well when they refuse to consider a Presidential claim of usurpation by Congress. And when they refuse to consider an individual claim of constitutional right, they abdicate their principal role, to ensure that the government carries out the purpose that, more than two hundred years ago, we declared to be a self-evident truth: "to secure these rights governments are instituted among men."

Whether the President has the power to terminate a treaty of the United States; whether a particular agreement negotiated by the President is a treaty requiring Senate consent; whether a particular military action is a war, which only Congress can make; whether a legislative act or an executive action deprives individuals of liberty or property without due process of law—these are difficult questions requiring for their resolution careful reading of text, original intent, grand design, history, and ideology: they are questions susceptible of resolution only in context and often in the light of general guidelines to be drawn. But those questions are no more difficult than others that the courts have addressed, and the courts cannot avoid deciding them without betraying our constitutional ideology and the judicial role in maintaining it.

My difficulty with the political question doctrine in foreign affairs is not technical. Nor, I think, is it quixotic. I do not oppose judicial prudence or having the courts impose prudence on the rest of government. I am as impressed as anyone by Professor Alexander Bickel's elegant, sophisticated defense of the doctrine.[37] But it should not be applied at the expense of constitutionalism. It should not be interpreted and used by lower courts to avoid deciding constitutional issues, issues of usurpation, issues of federalism, issues of rights.

I am not suggesting that federal judges, contemporary successors to the practical men that sat as courts of equity of old, should issue orders to end a war or drop (or not drop) a bomb. We have entrusted those decisions to Congress and the President, and nothing in our constitutionalism requires or warrants judicial second guesses on such issues. A court should not declare a question political and nonjusticiable when what the court means to say is that the particular exercise of authority by one of the political branches is within the constitutional authority of that branch, as half the courts held in the Vietnam cases and as courts might have held in other cases. In such cases, the court should affirm the exercise of authority by Congress or President; it should not dismiss the issue as nonjusticiable.

Even when there is a constitutional issue, I agree, equitable discretion might shape the remedy. But even if a remedy were denied or delayed, a judgment declaring what constitutionalism and our democracy require will diffuse tensions in the twilight zone between President and Congress and reduce frictions under the treaty power; it will shore up individual rights where they are particularly vulnerable, e.g., to patriotic passions.

The courts need new guidance. Lower courts have incanted "political question" and *Baker* clauses ritually, as Learned Hand once said, as "anodynes for the pains of reasoning."[38] Courts of appeals have frequently rejected invocations of *Baker* or laid them aside, affirming on other grounds, but have not illuminated the political question doctrine or clarified the *Baker* formulations. What the lower courts have done only confirms the view that *Baker* is a confusion of constitutional truisms with prudential caveats that do not—and could not—mean what they seem to say. If it is textually demonstrable that an issue is committed to a coordinate political department, the issue is not for that reason nonjusticiable; the court should honor that textual commitment by adjudicating the question and finding that the political branch acted within its constitutional authority. Half the *Baker* guidelines are contradicted by the institution of judicial review itself. As regards constitutional questions, at least, a court cannot hide behind a lack of discoverable and manageable standards; it makes such judgments every day, distilling manageable, if not discoverable, standards—e.g., in deciding what is due process of law. A court expresses "lack of respect" to a coordinate branch and creates potential embarrassment daily when it scrutinizes political actions to assure that they are within constitutionally granted authority and that they do not infringe individual rights. Perhaps some of these jurisprudential caveats should guide the courts in determining what relief may be appropriately granted; they do not warrant a refusal to adjudicate.

It is time for the Supreme Court to revisit *Baker* and try again. At least, the Court should tell us what particular *Baker* clauses mean and why and in what context they may render a question nonjusticiable. Until the Court gives new guidance, one might attempt to unscramble the *Baker* formula into a set of simpler guidelines that will bring some order into lower court jurisprudence and perhaps, even, discourage frivolous litigation. I offer a few, with annotations.

a. A claim that an act of Congress is unconstitutional or that the President has exceeded his constitutional authority is in principle justiciable, not a "political question."

In fact, the powers of each political branch are large and, in adjudicating, the courts will generally find that Congress (or the President) acted within their authority. The Court might reasonably have so held in *Goldwater v. Carter* and in most—perhaps all—of the spate of war power cases since the Vietnam War in which the Government argued the political question doctrine and lower courts sometimes agreed. In a rare case the court might find that the executive branch (or even Congress) exceeded its authority and so declare.

b. A claim that the President acted beyond authority delegated by Congress, or contrary to legislative direction, is not a political question and is justiciable.

That applies regardless of the subject matter of the statute and includes legislation on war powers or covert activities.

Claims that the President has not complied with the War Powers Resolution, however, raise special difficulties. The resolution is not well drafted and does not do what the authors sought to do; it needs to be rewritten. The operative provisions of the act require consultation with and reporting to Congress, and, by the traditional learning, it is difficult to find standing for a member of Congress to complain of presidential failures in those respects and impossible to find standing for anyone else. Moreover, the circumstances requiring consultation and reporting are difficult to determine and difficult to appraise. For example, a claim that presidential deployment of forces is within the War Powers Resolution and requires consultation and reporting may depend on a determination as to whether the forces were to be involved in "hostilities" and whether such involvement is "imminent," determinations that may be beyond judicial competence. In other cases, too, the court may find itself unable to determine whether an executive act conforms to a constitutional or legislative mandate because information essential for such a determination is not provided by the plaintiff or is otherwise unavailable. The court need not adjudicate what it cannot properly adjudicate.

c. In every case the court must consider the appropriateness of the remedy sought or of any other remedy that may be available.

The court may refuse any remedy or a particular remedy for want of equity or from its inability to fashion a remedy that is appropriate. But it is not inappropriate to declare the law and postpone a remedy to be worked out by those involved. One may be acutely unhappy with the too deliberate speed of the implementation of *Brown v. Board of Education*[39] yet recognize that different constitutional deficiencies may require special remedies, tailored and even delayed. The political branches, authoritatively informed of a constitutional deficiency, can well help create their own remedies. The prudential caveats listed by the Supreme Court in *Baker* may be relevant here.

■ We have come a long way from the view that judicial review should be avoided if at all possible. The courts have established their authority, and they are not as vulnerable as was once thought. They are now invited by state and federal governments and by the political branches to resolve issues between them; they are urged daily by citizens to declare and protect their rights. "It is emphatically the province and duty of the judicial department to say what the law is."[40] In a famous statement, Charles Evans Hughes wrote: "We are under a Constitution, but the Constitution is what the judges say it is." So much is part of our skeptical folklore. But Hughes' sentence continued: "and the judiciary is the safeguard of our liberty and of our property under the Constitution."[41] It is also the safeguard of constitutionalism, of diffused power, and of representative democracy.

Commitment to judicial review, to the safeguarding of constitutionalism, ought to imbue also other judicial functions. Another day, another lecturer might well pursue other implications of the judicial role in a constitutional democracy.

4

FOREIGN AFFAIRS AND INDIVIDUAL RIGHTS

■

After two hundred years the United States is a constitutional democracy. In one respect *constitutional democracy* is an oxymoron: democracy is committed to government by the people, but constitutionalism implies limits on government, even on government by the people and their representatives. For the framers the principal limitation on government was implied in the requirement that it respect the constitutional blueprint, its republican institutions and processes, its separation of powers and checks and balances, and the allocations of its federal system. What that blueprint prescribed in those respects is now deeply rooted and taken for granted; it is not open to question and generates few issues. The principal constitutional limitation on government that is operative today is that government must respect the rights of the individual. Today constitutionalism is virtually synonymous with protection of rights, and the protection of individual rights forms the largest part of our constitutional jurisprudence.

The framers' generation was deeply committed to individual rights: "to secure these rights, governments are instituted among men" (see p. 4). Nothing in the framers' conception of rights suggested that

93

respect for individual rights should be less or different in the conduct of the foreign relations of the new republic. Two hundred years of national life and constitutional history have transformed individual rights in conception and content; in some respects, at least, individual rights now appear less or different where foreign affairs are involved.

The transformation of our rights generally has made them our hallmark and our pride. I am not persuaded that deviations or modifications in the respect for rights where foreign relations are concerned is necessary, desirable, or warranted. Such derogations are not consistent with our commitment to constitutionalism; they are not justified by our commitment to democracy.

Individual Rights Two Hundred Years Later

■ At the Constitutional Convention the framers did not include a bill of rights, principally because they did not think one would be necessary.[1] The new federal government they were creating would have limited powers and would therefore have little direct impact on the individual citizen in ways that might threaten his/her rights. For the individual, the principal government would continue to be the state government, and each state government was limited by the state constitution which reflected commitment to rights, several of them including prominently a bill of rights.

As the price of ratification of the United States Constitution, a bill of rights was promised, and the Bill of Rights was added by constitutional amendment in 1791. The framers of the Bill of Rights pressed for the series of rights that we know from what emerged. They did not articulate a theory of rights or set forth a comprehensive catalog of rights. They were aware that their bill of rights was not complete, hence the Ninth Amendment: "The enumeration in the Constitution of certain rights shall not be construed to disparage or deny others retained by the people." We do not know what other rights they were thinking about. As a bill of rights to be protected against the new federal government, perhaps its framers did not see it necessary to include rights that they did not imagine could be invaded by that new government of limited powers.* Perhaps it did not include "civil rights,"

---

*The Bill of Rights had to be established by constitutional amendment, a process that may have discouraged a more elaborate and complete catalog of rights.

which would be protected by state constitutions against state governments or which did not need explicit protection because they went without saying and were protected by the common law—the rights of personhood before the law, the right to own property, to make contracts, to bring suits, to marry a person of one's choice, to have or not have children and raise a family, to choose one's work and place of residence, to travel, to pursue an education.

As the framers may have anticipated, few issues arose under the Bill of Rights during most of our earlier history; none came to the Supreme Court before the Civil War.* But transformations in national life have brought corresponding transformations in constitutional jurisprudence. A major reconstitution followed the Civil War when the Constitution was amended to abolish slavery, and the Fourteenth Amendment effectively nationalized rights giving the federal government the responsibility and the power to protect rights against violation by the states. Explicitly, that amendment commanded the states to provide due process of law and the equal protection of the laws for all; in time—much later—the Supreme Court held that the amendment rendered virtually all the protections of the Bill of Rights applicable to the states as well.[3]

We have also recognized the need to give constitutional protection to rights that the framers apparently took for granted. The framers knew their civil rights and were secure in them (under the common law) and may not have felt the need to give them constitutional status or even to make them explicit. Four score years later, the emancipation of the slaves brought into society a large group of persons whose personal and civil rights could not be taken for granted. It may be that the framers of the Fourteenth Amendment thought they were only assuring to blacks what others had enjoyed, the basic, undeniable human rights of all individuals, which, for the new citizens, could not be left to the protection of state constitutions, state governments, and state courts. But the Fourteenth Amendment did not enumerate those rights, referring only generally to "privileges and immunities" and to "due process of law," and relying on the requirement of equal protection of the laws to assure to all whatever rights the majority had long

---

*I do not include the Dred Scott case in which, in 1857, the Supreme Court held that the act of Congress that freed a slave if his master brought him into a free state violated the Fifth Amendment because it deprived the master of his property without due process of law.[2] The Alien and Sedition Laws enacted by Congress towards the end of the eighteenth century were short lived and did not reach the Supreme Court.

enjoyed. Immediately after the Civil War, Congress enacted civil rights acts to safeguard for blacks civil rights that white inhabitants had enjoyed, though not mentioned in the Bill of Rights; again, a century later, in the 1960s, Congress enacted a new series of civil rights acts to assure to the disadvantaged what others had long enjoyed. But Congress, too, did not purport to enumerate all of a person's rights: some civil rights acts refer to rights safeguarded by the Constitution, which requires that we determine which rights are protected by the Constitution and that we find rights in the Constitution if they are to enjoy statutory protection.

Except for the right to vote we have not added explicitly to the rights protected by the Constitution, but individual claims, imaginative counsel, and judicial exegesis have transformed rights probably beyond what the framers of the Bill of Rights, and even the framers of the Fourteenth Amendment, would have recognized. The growth and proliferation of rights and their protection by the courts and by Congress have not been steady and linear; after the amendments and civil rights acts that constituted the peace treaty of the Civil War, significant growth did not occur until the decades between world wars and rapid growth only after the Second World War.

Most impressive has been the expansion of our eighteenth-century rights in both conception and content. We have opened our Constitution to every man and woman, to new rights and to new conceptions of old rights, beyond rights rooted in individual freedom to rights rooted in individual dignity and worth. We have established political rights for all, and we have moved beyond political rights to civil and personal rights, beyond liberty to greater equality and less inequality. We now safeguard not only political freedom but personal, social, and sexual freedom, and we have recognized a zone of autonomy—the new privacy—in which the individual is free to make his or her choices. We have moved from the right of assembly to a right of association and to freedom not to associate; from nonestablishment of religion to a wall of separation between church and state. The privacy of the home and the freedom from unreasonable search and seizure have been extended to the office and the automobile, to wherever one has come to expect and value some freedom from intrusion.

Perhaps the greatest expansion has been in the rights of those accused of crime. The framers, I think, were concerned to protect the respectable and the innocent, the political or religious dissident, against governmental oppression. Today we believe that even the worst of us have rights—to fair trial, to counsel (provided by government for those who cannot provide their own), to freedom from self-incrimination. Punishment that is excessive is now cruel and unusual, and the death penalty has been sharply curtailed. We have refined the equal protection of the laws, recognizing certain classifications—notably race—as suspect. Once closed categories are now open. Prisoners now have rights, as do military personnel, mental patients, pupils in the schools, and children independently of their parents. Growth brought also homogenization of rights in relation to both federal and state governments so that today, in the face of constitutional text, original intent, and history, the individual enjoys virtually the same safeguards for the same rights against both federal and state governments.

The explosion of rights I have described may promise yet more, for it confirms the essentially open character of our Constitution, as always subject to continuing synthesis of immutable principle with contemporary values. Old assumptions have been reexamined and stereotypes penetrated, not least the place and role and talents of women. Conceptions of public morals have been narrowed; those about the general welfare have been expanded.

Perhaps the inevitable consequence of expanding and proliferating rights was the clear emergence of the principle of "balancing" individual liberty and public interest to determine the limits of each. Although the courts do not attend seriously to objections that economic and social regulation limits individual autonomy or liberty, in principle — for us as for the framers—all governmental action must justify itself as a means rationally linked to some public purpose. But rights are not absolute and in some times and circumstances virtually every right might give way to some other public good. Some individual rights and freedoms, however—speech, press, assembly, religion, old and new privacy, freedom from racial discrimination—are fundamental and preferred, and invasions of such rights are suspect and will be sharply scrutinized and sustained only for a compelling interest (which the courts find only rarely).

I have been discussing the rights we now have as higher law, regardless of the will of majorities and of their representatives and officials. But the Fourteenth Amendment, and the commerce and "spending" powers of Congress, in particular, have enabled the courts to unleash and even encourage Congress and state legislatures to expand individual rights and to add new protections—for the right to vote, for freedom from private discrimination on grounds of race or gender, for "the right to know" as by freedom of information acts.

Rights In Foreign Affairs

■ Foreign affairs are not a constitutional category, and nothing in the original Constitution or in the amendments suggests that they apply in lesser degree, or differently, to foreign affairs. In principle, then, individual rights are protected against excesses in the conduct of foreign as in domestic affairs. But in fact, the protection of individual rights in the governance of foreign affairs looks and is different.

Foreign affairs have not loomed large in the jurisprudence of rights. Principally, the conduct of foreign relations does not commonly impinge directly on the individual in ways that would implicate his/her protected rights, and our jurisprudence would not give an individual standing to object to the bulk of foreign policy activity. Where an act of Congress or an executive act related to foreign affairs impinges on an individual's rights, habits of mind in both the political branches and the courts have foreclosed or mitigated or discouraged scrutiny; the political question doctrine, in particular, has been invoked to foreclose judicial review.* When the courts do review, doctrines that provide for balancing individual rights against public interest find individual rights often depreciated and public interest sometimes exaggerated.

The authoritative Restatement of the Foreign Relations Law of the United States concluded recently: "The provisions of the United States Constitution safeguarding individual rights generally control the United States government in the conduct of its foreign relations as well as in domestic matters, and generally limit governmental authority whether it is exercised in the United States or abroad, and whether such authority is exercised unilaterally or by international agreement."[4]

That the conduct of foreign affairs is subject to constitutional restraints was not always recognized. In 1958, however, the Court explicitly assured us that "[t]he restrictions confining Congress in the exercise of any of the powers expressly delegated to it in the Constitution apply with equal vigor when that body seeks to regulate our

---

*It may also have encouraged the political branches not to look closely at national laws and policies for possible violations of individual rights.

relations with other nations. . . ."[5] The Court there affirmed the applicability of constitutional limitations to powers "expressly delegated . . . in the Constitution"; there is nothing to suggest that constitutional restrictions apply with less vigor when Congress (or the executive) acts under powers not expressly delegated by the framers but which the Court later found to be inherent in the international sovereignty of the United States.[6]

Constitutional restrictions and prohibitions apply equally to treaties of the United States. Earlier in this century the myth was extant that the United States could make treaties without regard to constitutional restraints, and the political branches sometimes acted as though other international agreements or acts of the United States were similarly immune. That myth was exploded in 1957. Justice Black said: "The prohibitions of the Constitution were designed to apply to all branches of the National Government and they cannot be nullified by the Executive or by the Executive and Senate combined."[7]

Treaties, acts of Congress, and executive actions in foreign affairs are subject to constitutional safeguards for individual rights, in foreign as in domestic matters. There are issues of individual rights that are intrinsically and particularly foreign policy related: claims by persons outside the United States, whether citizens of the United States or of other countries; issues of immigration and deportation; some issues of nationalization and the treatment of aliens.*

■ *The Constitution Abroad.* In the opinion I have cited, Justice Black also said: "The United States is entirely a creature of the Constitution. . . . It can only act in accordance with all the limitations imposed by the Constitution." And: "[C]onstitutional protections for the individual were designed to restrict the United States Government when it acts outside of this country, as well as here at home."[8]

Justice Black's principle suggests a conception of the Constitution that the Court did not accept earlier in our history. Once, some Justices thought the Constitution was a local contract only.[9] There is every reason to believe that Justice Black's conception was that of the framers. Jefferson's declaration proclaimed the rights of all men—all human beings—everywhere, not only of white settlers on the North American

---

*During the next century we will doubtless be inquiring increasingly into the relevance for our jurisprudence of international human rights standards.

continent. But in the nineteenth century, thanks perhaps to rising isolationism and xenophobia, we sometimes lost sight of our universal human rights ideology. With regret, if not dismay, we now read the Justices who wrote: "By the Constitution a government is ordained and established 'for the United States of America'. . . . The Constitution can have no operation in another country."* The Court, I think, fabricated that conclusion out of whole cloth foreign to Jefferson and the framers. They did indeed ordain and establish a constitution for the new United States of America. But it was a constitution "for the United States" as a new national entity, not for its territory, as it was then or was to be later. Nothing in the Constitution or in the framers' conceptions suggested that they had in mind any territorial limitations.

For Justice Black, the Constitution did not merely protect United States citizens against abuse of their rights by government. It was not only a social contract by citizens for citizens. It was not only for home consumption. It established a community of conscience and righteousness and the people directed their representatives to respect individual human rights wherever they exercised the people's authority, in or outside the United States, and no matter in relation to whom that authority was exercised.[10] In the United States, then, aliens enjoy constitutional protection against both the federal and state governments essentially to the same extent as do United States citizens.[11] When the United States exercises authority on the high seas, as when its officials stop vessels suspected of smuggling persons or goods into the United States, their actions are subject to the limitations of the Fourth Amendment against unreasonable search and seizures and those of the Fifth Amendment protecting life, liberty, or property against deprivation without due process of law or prohibiting the taking of property for public use without just compensation.[12] When courts are

---

*The Court made that declaration denying the protections of the Constitution to Ross, a seaman on a United States vessel tried for murder in a United States consular court. During the same era and its ungenerous jurisprudential mood, the Court in *Ker v. Illinois* held that a person kidnapped abroad by United States officials could nevertheless be brought to trial in the United States. Thirty years ago the Court dismissed *Ross* as "a relic from a different era." *Ker* is from that same era but is still flourishing. The *Chinese Exclusion Case*, in effect excluding immigration from constitutional control, is also a relic of that era, also, alas, flourishing. In re *Ross*, 140 U.S. 453 (1891); *Ker v. Illinois*, 119 U.S. 436 (1886); *Chinese Exclusion Case*, 130 U.S. 581 (1889). See also L. Henkin, "The Constitution and United States Sovereignty: A Century of *Chinese Exclusion* and Its Progeny," *Harv. L. Rev.* (1987), 100: 853.

On the other hand, during the same period the Court recognized the rights of alien Chinese in the United States to full constitutional protection and the equal protection of the laws. *Yick Wo v. Hopkins,* 118 U.S. 356 (1886). "The Fourteenth Amendment to the Constitution is not confined to the protection of citizens." *Id.,* 118 U.S. at 369. Cf. *Barbier v. Connolly,* 113 U.S. 27 (1885).

held in a foreign country under the authority of the United States, the United States must provide the safeguards required in the criminal process, notably a jury trial and a right to counsel, perhaps even trial before a judge whose independence is protected by life tenure.[13] Even the women of Greenham Common in England may claim constitutional restraints on the acts of United States officials that affect them.*

■ *Immigration and Deportation.* The history we bring into our third century is grossly deficient for protecting rights in one major respect related to our external relations. Long ago, before the courts became sensitive to the demands of rights and helped make them flourish, the Supreme Court decided in effect that the Constitution provides no protection in the immigration process to applicants from abroad and not much more to aliens already in the United States. The Court would not listen to substantive objections to the immigration laws even when they blatantly discriminated on grounds of race and religion or when they excluded both would-be immigrants and visitors on account of their political views.[14] The United States has encouraged naturalization, and the Court has now recognized that citizenship once acquired cannot be taken away,[15] but if an alien does not seek naturalization, under prevailing doctrine that the Court has refused to reexamine, the alien, though lawfully resident in the United States, could be deported for any reason or no reason.[16] Aliens not lawfully admitted but physically present can be detained indefinitely for no reason better than that there is no country to which we can deport them or to which they can go voluntarily.[17] And United States nationals cannot assert a right to exercise their freedom of thought and expression and their right of assembly by inviting foreign scholars they wished to hear.[18]

■ *Aliens in the United States.* We have been generous—and more generous than other countries—in our treatment of aliens. The Court has read the provision in the Fourteenth Amendment that states shall

---

*Early in this century the Court held that the Constitution applies in full vigor in territories that Congress incorporated but not in those unincorporated. The "Insular Cases": *Downes v. Bidwell,* 182 U.S. 244 (1901); *Hawaii v. Mankichi,* 190 U.S. 197 (1903); *Dorr v. United States,* 195 U.S. 138 (1904); *Balzac v. Porto Rico,* 258 U.S. 298 (1922). That distinction has not been reexamined and in time became less significant as the United States granted independence to, or incorporated, unincorporated territories.

not deny to any person the equal protection of the laws as forbidding the states to exclude alien children from public education even if these aliens had not been lawfully admitted to this country.[19] The Constitution does not permit states to deny resident aliens an equal opportunity to practice a profession or seek employment, including public employment. But the state may exclude resident aliens from "participation in its democratic political institutions," and the courts have permitted the states an extravagant view of governance, of "important public responsibility," allowing them, for example, to exclude noncitizens from serving as state troopers or secondary school teachers.[20] The Court has also been unwilling to read the Constitution as denying the federal government authority to discriminate against aliens, in part from a notion of early date that the United States should be able to use our treatment of aliens as chips for bargaining with foreign governments as to how they treat United States nationals.[21]

■ *Individual Rights and Public Interest.* It may be that the framers had a narrower conception of rights or defined particular rights more restrictively. As so defined, they may have seen our rights as absolute. Justice Hugo Black insisted that when the First Amendment declares that "Congress shall make no law . . . abridging the freedom of speech," that meant *no law,* and others agreed. But perhaps inevitably, that required them to adopt more restrained interpretations of "abridging" or of "the freedom of speech." Our jurisprudence has largely avoided trying to recapture the framers' conceptions and struggling with such parsings of individual phrases in the First Amendment or in other provisions of the Bill of Rights. Instead, in several contexts, we have developed a principle of "balancing" individual rights and public good. The individual counts and individual life, liberty, and property have to be taken into account in any exercise of governmental power, but the public need may sometimes override the individual right. Some rights, however, are fundamental or preferred and can be outweighed only by a compelling public interest. A similar balancing often takes place when we decide whether a particular arrest or search and seizure is "unreasonable" (and prohibited by the Fourth Amendment), perhaps whether a particular punishment is cruel or unusual (and prohibited by the Eighth Amendment). We may be involved in such balancing when we interpret other clauses, for example, in deciding whether some act of government is or is not a prohibited "abridgement" of a freedom under the First Amendment or a "deprivation" of "liberty" or "property" protected by due process or a "taking" of property requiring just compensation or even what the Fifth Amendment means when it provides that a person shall not be "compelled" in any criminal case to be a witness against himself.

Whatever the framers intended, balancing is now intrinsic to our protection of rights. But we cannot be loyal to the principles of constitutionalism if that balancing is done without due account to the individual right or with undue weight to the "public interest." We have not been sufficiently mindful of our constitutionalism in addressing the impact on individual rights of our foreign affairs. There is nothing in the framers' commitment to individual rights, in their—and our—commitment to constitutionalism, that would tolerate the conclusion that "[m]atters intimately related to foreign policy and national security are rarely proper subjects for judicial intervention"[22] or that would support the "traditional deference to executive judgment '[i]n this vast external realm'. . . ."[23] There is no balancing when every weight is given to what is in one balance and little to the other or when the courts will not even hold and read the balances.

In principle, then, the Bill of Rights and other constitutional safeguards for individual rights apply and are to be given effect in foreign relations as in domestic matters. But in the interpretation and application of particular rights and in the balancing of rights and public interest that has become the mode and mood for applying the requirements of substantive due process of law, foreign affairs have been "different," and individual rights have suffered. In the attitudes of abstention and deference quoted, I note, the Court virtually excludes from its review any matter "intimately related" to foreign policy. It begins—and too often ends—with deference to executive judgment in everything that is within "this vast external realm," regardless of the importance of any right involved or the lack of importance of the foreign policy invoked.* In foreign affairs, the private right gets comparatively short shrift; the public interest receives undue deference and

---

*I lay aside invasions of individual rights during war, such as the relocation and internment of persons of Japanese ancestry during the Second World War. Korematsu v. United States, 323 U.S. 214 (1944). There was even less justification when foreign policy, dressed as national security, was invoked, with little scrutiny and hardly any balancing, to invade important individual rights during periods of fearful reaction to the political threat of communism. In those cases, there was little scrutiny and balancing by the political branches and scrutiny and balancing by the courts was also sometimes little and often late.

extravagant weight often without meaningful scrutiny. The courts seem to continue to assume that everything plausibly related to foreign relations implicates important national interests and even national security. Even fundamental rights that are generally preferred and will bow only rarely and only to a compelling public interest, in foreign affairs are sometimes sacrificed, on the basis of unexamined assumptions, to interests that appear hardly compelling. And the tendency of courts to seek to shirk the duty to hear cases seems to deny rights that would be vindicated if the courts heard them.[24]

Fortunately, some claim of rights occasionally commends itself to the Supreme Court for the respect it deserves. The Court honored the heavy presumption against prior restraints on publication and refused to enjoin publication of the "Pentagon Papers," although they clearly and heavily implicated foreign affairs.[25] In 1988, it abandoned assumptions at least half a century old and held that picketing of a foreign embassy, at least on some subjects, at least at substantial distances, was protected by the freedom of expression.[26] In other cases involving other rights and other foreign policy claims, however, judicial deference takes over. For example, the Court has declared that "The right to travel is a part of the 'liberty' of which the citizen cannot be deprived without due process of law. . . . Freedom of movement is basic in our scheme of values."[27] Hence a citizen cannot be denied the right to travel in the United States because of his or her political opinions. But the Court held the right to travel abroad is less weighty than the right to travel within the United States, and that the Secretary of State may revoke a passport — and thereby effectively prevent travel abroad — when the Secretary concludes that an individual's activities abroad are likely to cause serious damage to the "national security or foreign policy" of the United States.[28] Surely, not everything that comes within "foreign policy," within that "vast external realm" is a compelling public interest that outweighs a freedom that is "basic in our scheme of values." Judicial deference and the "principle" that such matters are "rarely proper subjects for judicial intervention" will hardly assure the balancing required by our contemporary version of our ancestors' commitments.

■ Rights have flourished in the United States beyond recognition by the framers of either the Bill of Rights or the Civil War amendments, and the United States sees itself and is seen by others as a rights-ridden society. The political branches of government recognize and accept the limitations of rights on their governance. The courts effectively monitor respect for rights, and judicial protection for rights is commonly seen as the principal purpose and need for judicial review.

Few would claim that our jurisprudence of rights is now complete, but after two hundred years we have realized better the promises of the Declaration of Independence to which the framers were committed. We have a way to go. We might ask, too, whether we have not expanded or should not expand our conceptions of individual rights beyond those of the framers, notably to include a right for every person to meet his or her basic human needs in a free market society that is also a welfare society.

Constitutionalism implies respect for individual rights, and foreign affairs — like other national affairs — are not exempt from paying that respect. Democracy too owes such respect, and a democratic foreign policy also has to be sensitive to individual rights. In fact, since so much of our foreign affairs is less subject to the safeguards of separation of powers, of checks and balances, and of federalism, and since in the conduct of foreign affairs our representatives are less responsive and less accountable, the claims of individual rights are in risk of being sacrificed. The courts can monitor better than they do. We the citizens have to care and watch and sensitize our representatives to the security of our rights, since "to ensure these rights, governments are instituted among men."

5

A FINAL WORD

■

Bicentennials are the product of our penchant or need for celebration (and of our commitment to the decimal system). They provide an occasion for taking stock. A bicentennial of a constitution that has hardly been amended might well be a time to ask whether it needs tuning, if not a replacement of parts. The dictum "if it ain't broke . . ." applies here as elsewhere, but whether a constitution is "broke" in some respects may not always be apparent to a patient, perhaps inert, people, at least until there is a crisis.

I have addressed constitutional issues between President and Congress in the light of an inadequate text and what time has done to the uncertain intent of the framers. I have concluded that there is no need for radical constitutional surgery or treatment as regards foreign affairs in particular, but suggested that, where appropriate, we be guided in constitutional construction by principles of constitutionalism and democracy. I have considered the friction between the President and the Senate in the exercise of the treaty power and asked how international agreements should be made in a constitutional democracy.

These issues, too, do not cry for radical structural remedies. Like the tensions between President and Congress in the exercise of powers of war and peace and covert activities, those of the treaty power can be managed if Congress leads the President into regular arrangements and procedures of advice and consent that will assure that separation of powers and checks and balances result in cooperation rather than friction, in wiser action rather than in frustration or recrimination. The courts can contribute importantly by playing—confidently, firmly, wisely—the part in our constitutional governance to which the framers pointed and which history has established: umpiring the separation of powers and monitoring the bounds between public need and individual right.

In foreign affairs, I have concluded, it has become important to rededicate ourselves to the principles of constitutionalism—to limited, checked, balanced government and respect for law and individual rights. In foreign affairs we are particularly susceptible to the claims of "efficiency" at the expense of other values, to pleas that we repose full faith in "the experts," to demands of individual sacrifice, including the sacrifice of our obligation to scrutinize and criticize, and sacrifice of individual rights. In foreign affairs we are particularly susceptible to becoming bemused by assertion of "leadership," by appeal to false patriotism, by play on our fears of appearing divided before the world.

In particular, I have suggested, this Bicentennial invites us to ask whether our constitutional blueprint is appropriate to the democracy we have become. There is no single blueprint required to satisfy democracy in principle. I do not suggest that we consider moving to a different kind of democratic government, say to a parliamentary system, with or without proportional representation. Within our existing congressional-presidential system, it may indeed be desirable to consider constitutional change: A four-year term for the House? A longer term for Presidents? Modification of the electoral system for the presidency? * These and other such changes would, of course, have consequences for the constitutional law of foreign affairs as well.

In some respects, the two-hundred-year-old institutions we have, now based on universal suffrage, may well satisfy even some Platonic ideal of democracy. I hope that others will be moved to explore whether in our governance generally the old blueprint, now supported by universal suffrage, provides not merely inert acquiescence and a biennial-quadrennial plebiscite, but authentic participation, representation, responsibility, responsiveness, and accountability. Perhaps, without formal amendment but by constitutional adaptation between the polit-

---

* My own candidate for change would reverse Supreme Court interpretations of the Constitution that have prevented effective control of campaign expenditures and have in effect introduced a major property requirement as a condition of holding elective office.

ical branches with some judicial guidance, we can reshape institutions and institute procedures that will adjust old machinery to new ideology.

As regards the conduct of foreign affairs in particular, constitutional uncertainties, constitutional politics, and judicial abdication have raised the question whether in major respects the old blueprint provides a process that is authentically democratic and authentically constitutionalist. I have not concluded that there is a need for major, formal constitutional change. I do believe that, "where fairly possible," the Constitution should be construed so as to compel cooperation and safeguard rights.

Macaulay once said that our Constitution is "all sail and no anchor."[1] In foreign affairs, perhaps it is the rudder, too, that needs attention. In my view, rudder and anchor are in the charge of Congress. Congress has constitutional authority over navigation in the twilight zone between Congress and President; Congress can adjust the procedures for making treaties. Without formal amendment, with loyalty to text, to original intent, to history, the courts can calibrate our Constitution, and Congress can enact laws and develop institutions so as to reaffirm our ancestral commitment to constitutionalism appropriate to our democracy, in a nuclear world in the twenty-first century, the third century of the Constitution.

NOTES

■

Introduction

1. Gladstone, "Kin Beyond Sea," *N. Am. Rev.* 185 (1878), 127:185.

2. C. Beard and M. Beard, *The Rise of American Civilization* (rev. ed., New York: Macmillan, 1933), p. 317.

3. *Youngstown Sheet & Tube Co. v. Sawyer,* 343 U.S. 579, 635 (1952).

4. Hamilton, J. Madison, J. Jay, *The Federalist Papers,* no. 78 (New York: New American Library, 1961).

5. Lord Bolingbroke, "A Dissertation upon Parties" (1733–1734), in *The Works of Lord Bolingbroke* (1841), 2:88, quoted in C. H. McIlwain, *Constitutionalism: Ancient and Modern* (Ithaca: Cornell University Press, 1947), 3. See also Aristotle Book III, c. vi, § 1, of *The Politics,* where he defines a constitution as "the organization of a polis, in respect of its offices generally, but especially in respect of that particular office which is sovereign in all issues." Later in Book IV, c. i, § 9, he more fully defines it as "an organization of offices in a state, by which the method of their distribution is fixed, the sovereign authority is determined, and the nature of the end to be pursued by the association and all its members is prescribed." E. Barker, ed., *The Politics of Aristotle* (Oxford: Clarendon Press, 1946), pp. 110, 156.

6. Resolution of May 10, 1776, in *Journals of the Continental Congress* (Ford, ed. 1906), 4:342.

7. L. Henkin, *The Rights of Man Today* (Boulder, Colo.: Westview Press, 1978), ch. 2.

8. See, for example, P. L. Strauss, "Formal and Functional Approaches to Separation-of-Powers Questions — A Foolish Inconsistency?" *Cornell L. Rev.* (1987), 72:488.

9. This was one of the complaints of the anti-Federalists. See generally ch. 6, "The Aristocratic Tendency of the Constitution," in H. J. Storing, ed., *What the Anti-Federalists Were For* (Chicago: University of Chicago Press, 1981).

10. R. L. Schuyler, *The Constitution of the United States* (New York: Macmillan, 1923), p. 138.

11. Wood, "Democracy and the Constitution," in R. Goldwin and W. Schambra, eds., *How Democratic Is the Constitution?* (Washington, D.C.: American Enterprise Institute for Public Policy Research, 1980), p. 16.

12. The Voting Rights Act Amendments of 1970, § 201, 42 U.S.C. § 1973b. The Supreme Court upheld the power of Congress to do so. *Oregon v. Mitchell,* 400 U.S. 112 (1970).

13. See *Reynolds v. Sims,* 377 U.S. 533 (1964), and *Wesberry v. Sanders,* 376 U.S. 1 (1964).

14. Burke, Letter to the Sheriffs of Bristol, on the Affairs of America, April 3, 1777, in *The Works of Edmund Burke* (1869), vol. 2.

1. Tension in the Twilight Zone: Congress and the President

1. See generally ch. 1 of L. Henkin, *Foreign Affairs and the Constitution* (New York: Norton, 1975); see also ch. 9.

2. J. Rogers, *World Policing and the Constitution* (Boston: World Peace Foundation, 1945), p. 14.

3. *United States v. Curtiss-Wright Export Corp.,* 299 U.S. 304 (1936).

4. The phrase is Justice Jackson's. *Youngstown Sheet and Tube Co. v. Sawyer,* 343 U.S. 579, 641 (1952) (Jackson, J., concurring).

5. Jefferson, too, hardly an exponent of expansive constitutional construction of large presidential power, wrote: "The transaction of business with foreign nations is *Executive altogether.* It belongs, then, to the head of that department except as to such portions of it as are specially submitted to the Senate. "Exceptions are to be construed strictly" (T. Jefferson, *Writings,* (P. L. Ford, ed. (New York: Putnam, 1892), 5:162 [emphasis in original]).

6. Motion by James Madison and Elbridge Gerry. See Max Farrand, ed., *The Records of the Federal Convention of 1787,* (New Haven: Yale University Press, 1937), 2:318.

7. The Court seemed to treat the executive power clause as a source of

authority for the President to remove officers, compare *Myers v. United States,* 272 U.S. 52, 128 (1926), but nowhere considered it as a source of authority in foreign affairs. But see *Youngstown Sheet & Tube Co. v. Sawyer,* 343 U.S. 579, 641 (J. Jackson, concurring).

8. *United States v. Curtiss-Wright Export Corp.,* 299 U.S. 304, 320 (1936).

9. T. Roosevelt, *An Autobiography* (New York: Macmillan, 1913), pp. 371–372.

10. *Cong. Rec.* 7044 (1942), quoted and discussed in Corwin, *The President* (New York: New York University Press, 1957), pp. 250–252.

11. *Youngstown Sheet & Tube Co. v. Sawyer,* 343 U.S. 579, 637 (1952) (J. Jackson, concurring).

12. 50 U.S.C. §§ 1541–1548 (1989).

13. Veto Message, War Powers Resolution, by President Richard Nixon, October 24, 1973, *Cong. Q. Weekly Rep.,* 31:2855. The veto was overridden by Congress on November 7, 1973, *Cong. Rec.,* 119:36198, 36221.

14. *McCulloch v. Maryland,* 17 U.S. (4 Wheat.) 316, 407 (1819) (emphasis in original).

2. Treaties in a Constitutional Democracy

1. See *Edwards v. Carter,* 580 F. 2d 1055 (D.C. Cir.), *cert. denied,* 436 U.S. 907 (1978).

2. See A. Bestor, "Respective Roles of Senate and President in the Making and Abrogation of Treaties — The Original Intent of the Framers of the Constitution Historically Examined," *Wash. L. Rev.* (1979), 55:1; *The Federalist Papers,* no. 64 (Jay).

3. See L. Henkin, *Foreign Affairs and the Constitution* (New York: Norton, 1975), p. 132; compare W. Thayer, *The Life and Letters of John Hay* (Boston: Houghton Mifflin, 1915), 2:170.

4. See, e.g., the Senate conditions in two well-known instances, the 1950 Niagara Power Treaty with Canada and the Genocide Convention to which the Senate consented in 1986. On the former, see L. Henkin, *Foreign Affairs and the Constitution* (New York: Norton, 1972), pp. 134–135.

5. *United States v. Belmont,* 301 U.S. 324 (1937); *United States v. Pink,* 315 U.S. 203 (1942); *Dames & Moore v. Regan,* 453 U.S. 654 (1981).

6. See S. Res. 85, 91st Cong., 1st Sess., *Cong. Rec.* (1969), 115:17245.

7. S. Res. 536, 95th Cong., 2d Sess. (1978). See T. Franck and M. Glennon, *Foreign Relations and National Security Law, Cases and Materials* (St. Paul: West, 1987), pp. 396–399.

8. *Restatement (Third) Foreign Relations Law of the United States* § 302;

Reid v. Covert, 354 U.S. 1 (1957) (opinion of Black, J.); *Missouri v. Holland*, 252 U.S. 416 (1920); *Edwards v. Carter*, note 1 above.

9. *Myers v. United States*, 272 U.S. 52, 293 (1926).

3. The Courts in Foreign Affairs

1. *The Federalist Papers*, no. 78.

2. See Justice Robert Jackson's *The Struggle for Judicial Supremacy* (New York: Knopf, 1941). On a later occasion, he reminded his colleagues: "We are not final because we are infallible, but we are infallible only because we are final" (J. Jackson, concurring in *Brown v. Allen*, 344 U.S. 443, 540 [1953]).

3. E.g., *Regan v. Wald*, 468 U.S. 222 (1984).

4. See *Haig v. Agee*, 453 U.S. 280, 306 (1981); see also *Regan v. Wald*, note 3 above, citing *Califano v. Aznavorian*, 439 U.S. 170, 176 (1978).

5. A sad example is *Shaughnessy v. United States ex rel. Mezei*, 345 U.S. 206 (1953), where the court upheld the power of Congress to exclude a resident alien returning to the United States without a hearing and on the basis of confidential information. In 1985, the Court had an opportunity to reconsider that decision, but only two dissenting Justices seized that opportunity. See *Jean v. Nelson*, 472 U.S. 846 (1985) (Marshall and J.J. Brennan, dissenting).

6. We commonly credit John Marshall in *Marbury v. Madison*, 5 U.S. (1 Cranch) 137 (1803).

7. See *Ashwander v. TVA*, 297 U.S. 288, 346 (1936).

8. Correspondences of the Justices (1793), in H. Johnston, ed., *Correspondence and Public Papers of John Jay*, (New York: Putnam, 1891), 3:486–489.

9. See *Hayburn's Case*, 2 Dall. 409, 1 L.Ed. 436 (U.S. 1792).

10. See generally G. Gunther, ed., *Constitutional Law, Cases and Materials*, 11th ed. (Mineola, N.Y.: Foundation Press, 1985), ch. 11.

11. *Goldwater v. Carter*, 444 U.S. 996 (1979); *Edwards v. Carter*, 580 F.2d 1055 (D.C. Cir.), *cert. denied*, 436 U.S. 907 (1978); *Dole v. Carter*, 569 F.2d 1109 (10th Cir. 1977); *Crockett v. Reagan*, 720 F.2d 1355 (D.C. Cir. 1983), *cert. denied*, 467 U.S. 1251 (1984); *Lowry et al. v. Reagan*, Order of Oct. 17, 1988, No. 87–5426 (D.C. Cir. 1988); *Conyers v. Reagan*, 578 F. Supp. 324 (D.D.C. 1984); *Cranston v. Reagan, et, al.*, 611 F. Supp. 247 (D.D.C. 1985).

12. E.g., *Hammer v. Dagenhart*, 247 U.S. 251 (1918); *Carter v. Carter Coal Co.*, 298 U.S. 238 (1936); *Massachusetts v. Mellon*, 262 U.S. 447 (1923).

13. E.g., *Youngstown Steel & Tube Co. v. Sawyer*, 343 U.S. 579 (1952).

14. "Is There a 'Political Question' Doctrine?," *Yale L. J.* (1976), 85:597.

15. 369 U.S. 186 (1962).

16. *Id.* at 217.

17. E.g., *Committee of U.S. Citizens Living in Nicaragua v. Reagan*, 859 F.2d 929, 932 (D.C. Cir. 1988) ("reliance on the political question doctrine was misplaced").

18. In 1984, the Supreme Court refused to dismiss as a political question a challenge to liability limitations under a treaty that were inconsistent with federal regulations *Trans World Airlines, Inc. v. Franklin Mint Corp.*, 466 U.S. 243 (1984).

In 1986, the Court rejected the "political question" argument in a challenge to an executive decision not to enforce whaling quotas against Japan, claimed to be required by statute. *Japan Whaling Ass'n v. American Cetacean Society*, 478 U.S. 221 (1986).

19. Compare *Gilligan v. Morgan*, 413 U.S. 1 (1973).

20. *Coleman v. Miller*, 307 U.S. 433 (1939).

21. 444 U.S. 996 (1979).

22. *Id.* at 1004 (footnote omitted).

23. *Id.* at 1006.

24. *Youngstown Sheet & Tube Co. v. Sawyer*, note 13 above.

25. *Buckley v. Valeo*, 424 U.S. 1 (1976) (Congressional exercise of power of appointment); *INS v. Chadha*, 462 U.S. (1983) (legislative veto); *Bowsher v. Synar*, 478 U.S. 714 (1986) (invalidating congressional control of Comptroller General); *Morrison v. Olson*, 487 U.S. 654, 108 S. Ct. 2597 (1988) (Congress may authorize judicial appointment of special prosecutor).

26. See my article, note 14 above, at p. 623.

27. *Conyers v. Reagan*, note 11 above; *Crockett, et al. v. Reagan*, note 11 above; *Sanchez-Espinoza, et al. v. Reagan*, 770 F.2d 202 (1985); *The Committee of U.S. Citizens Living in Nicaragua v. Reagan*, note 17 above; *Lowry et al. v. Reagan*, note 11 above.

28. See Henkin, "The Constitution as Compact and as Conscience," *Wm. & Mary L. Rev.* (1985), 27:11.

29. *Greenham Women Against Cruise Missiles v. Reagan*, 591 F. Supp. 1332 (S.D.N.Y. 1984).

30. *Dole v. Carter*, note 11 above.

31. *Americans United for the Separation of Church and State v. Reagan*, 786 F.2d 194 (3d Cir. 1986).

32. *Dickson v. Ford*, 521 F.2d 234 (5th Cir. 1975).

33. *Haitian Refugee Center, Inc. v. Gracey*, 600 F. Supp. 1396 (D.D.C. 1985).

34. *Ramirez de Arellano v. Weinberg*, 745 F.2d 1500 (D.C. Cir. 1984), vacated, 471 U.S. 1113 (1985).

35. Wechsler, "Toward Neutral Principles of Constitutional Law," *Harv. L. Rev.* (1959), 73:1.

36. *Cohens v. Virginia,* 19 U.S. (6 Wheat.) 264, 404 (1821).

37. A. Bickel, "The Supreme Court, 1960 Term—Foreword: The Passive Virtues," *Harv. L. Rev.* (1961), 75:40; A. Bickel, *The Least Dangerous Branch* (Indianapolis: Bobbs-Merrill, 1962), p. 172.

38. *Commissioner of Internal Revenue v. Sansome,* 60 F.2d 931, 933 (2d Cir. 1932).

39. *Brown v. Board of Education,* 349 U.S. 294 (1955).

40. *Marbury v. Madison,* 5 U.S. (1 Cranch) at 177; *Cooper v. Aaron,* 358 U.S. 1 (1958) (opinion by nine justices).

41. Speech at Elmira, May 3, 1907, in *Charles E. Hughes, Addresses* (1908) 139–141, quoted in *The Autobiographical Notes of Charles Evans Hughes,* D. Danelski and J. Tulchin, eds. (Cambridge: Harvard University Press, 1973), p. 144.

4. Foreign Affairs and Individual Rights

1. *The Federalist Papers,* no. 84. See also C. Pinckney, Speech in South Carolina House of Representatives, in M. Farrand, *The Records of the Federal Convention of 1787* (1911), 3:256.

2. *Dred Scott v. Sanford,* 60 U.S. 393 (1856).

3. *Duncan v. Louisiana,* 391 U.S. 145 (1968).

4. *Restatement (Third) Foreign Relations Law of the United States* § 721.

5. *Perez v. Brownell,* 356 U.S. 44, 58 (1958) (upholding a statute depriving a man of his citizenship for voting in a foreign election). In 1967, the Court overruled *Perez,* holding that the Constitution prohibits deprivation of citizenship, but not even the sharp dissent suggested that legislation relating to foreign affairs is not subject to constitutional limitations (*Afroyim v. Rusk,* 387 U.S. 253 [1967]).

6. *United States v. Curtiss-Wright Export Corp.,* 299 U.S. 304 (1936).

7. *Reid v. Covert,* 354 U.S. 1, 17 (1957) (plurality opinion).

8. *Id.,* 354 U.S. at 6–7 (footnotes omitted).

9. In re *Ross,* 140 U.S. 453 (1891).

10. L. Henkin, "The Constitution as Compact and as Conscience: Individual Rights Abroad and at Our Gates," *Wm. & Mary L. Rev.* (1985), 27:11.

11. Restatement, note 4 above, § 722.

12. See L. Henkin, "The Constitution at Sea," *Maine L. Rev.* (1984), 36:201.

13. Compare *U.S. v. Tiede,* 86 F.R.D. 227 (1979), with *United States ex rel. Toth v. Quarles,* 350 U.S. 11 (1955).

14. See The Immigration Act of 1924, ch. 190, 43 Stat. 153 (1924); Immigration and Nationality Act § 212 (A)(28), 8 U.S.C. § 1182 (27)-(29).

See also *Kleindienst v. Mandel*, 408 U.S. 753 (1972) (visitor); *Harisiades v. Shaughnessy*, 342 U.S. 580 (1952) (would-be immigrant).

15. *Afroyim v. Rusk*, note 5 above.

16. See Immigration and Nationality Act § 241, 8 U.S.C. § 1251, for a list of postentry acts that can serve as bases for deportation. See also chapter 5, "Deportation," in T. Aleinikoff and D. Martin, *Immigration: Process and Policy* (St. Paul: Martin, 1985).

17. *Garcia-Mir v. Meese*, 788 F.2d 1446 (11th Cir.), *cert. denied*, 479 U.S. 886 (1986). But cf. *Rodriguez-Fernandez v. Wilkinson*, 505 F. Supp. 787 (D. Kan. 1980), *aff'd*, 654 F.2d 1382 (10th Cir. 1981).

18. *Kleindienst v. Mandel*, note 14 above.

19. *Plyler v. Doe*, 457 U.S. 202 (1982).

20. *Foley v. Connelie*, 435 U.S. 291 (1978) (state troopers); *Ambach v. Norwick*, 441 U.S. 68 (1979) (schoolteachers).

21. Compare *Hampton v. Mow Sun Wong*, 426 U.S. 88 (1976): ". . . if the Congress or the President had expressly imposed the citizenship requirement, it would be justified by the national interest in providing an incentive for aliens to become naturalized, or possibly even as providing the President with an expendable token for treaty negotiating purposes. . . ." 426 U.S. at 105, with *Mathews v. Diaz*, 426 U.S. 67 (1976): "Since decisions in these matters may implicate our relations with foreign powers, and since a wide variety of classifications must be defined in light of changing political and economic circumstances, such decisions are frequently of a character more appropriate to either the Legislature or the Executive than to the Judiciary. This very case illustrates the need for flexibility in policy choices rather than the rigidity often characteristic of constitutional adjudication." 426 U.S. at 81.

22. *Haig v. Agee*, 453 U.S. 280, 292 (1981).

23. *Regan v. Wald*, 468 U.S. 222, 243 (1984) (quoting *U.S. v. Curtiss-Wright*, note 6 above.

24. See chapter 3, "The Courts in Foreign Affairs."

25. *New York Times Co. v. United States*, 403 U.S. 713 (1971).

26. *Boos v. Barry*, 485 U.S. 312, 108 S. Ct. 1157 (1988).

27. *Kent v. Dulles*, 357 U.S. 116, 125–126 (1958).

28. See *Haig v. Agee*, note 22 above, pp. 292, 306.

5. A Final Word

1. Letter to H. S. Randall, May 23, 1857, in G. O. Trevelyan, *The Life and Letters of Lord Macaulay* (New York: Harper, 1876), 2:409–410.

Index

■